Founded in 1964 by John Wa[...]

Voices: *Journal of the Americ[...]*

MW01114977

Editors:
  Kristin Staroba, MSW | *kristin.sta[...]*
  1201 Connecticut Ave., NW, Ste. 710
  Washington DC 20036
  Carla Bauer, LCSW   *crbauer01@bellsouth.net*
  2801 Buford Hwy NE, Ste. T-80
  Atlanta, GA 30329
Graphic Designer:
  Mary de Wit
Business Manager:
  Lisa Kays
  1800 R Street NW #C-8
  Washington, DC 20009
International Consultant:
  Jacob Megdell, PhD, Canada
Emeriti:
  Penelope L. Norton, PhD, *Immediate Past Editor*
  Doris Jackson, PhD, *Editor Emerita*
  Tom Burns, PhD, *Editor Emeritus*
  Jon Farber, PhD, *Editor Emeritus*
  Monique Savlin, PhD, *Editor Emerita*
  Edward Tick, PhD, *Editor Emeritus*
  E. Mark Stern, PhD, *Editor Emeritus*
  Vin Rosenthal, PhD, *Editor Emeritus*
Associates:
  Hallie S. Lovett, PhD, *Contributing Editor*
  Bob Rosenblatt, PhD, *Intervision Editor*
  Barry Wepman, PhD, *Poetry Editor*
  Ruth Wittersgreen, PhD, *Poetry Editor*

Lee Blackwell, PhD
Brooke Bralove, LCSW-C
Peggy Brooks, PhD
Grover Criswell, MDiv
Susan Diamond, MSW
Molly Donovan, PhD
Nicholas Emmanuel, LPC
Rhona Engels, ACSW
Stephanie Ezust, PhD
Pamela Finnerty, PhD
Natan Harpaz, PhD
Stephen Howard, MD
Susan Jacobson, MMH
Nicholas Kirsch, PhD
Judy Lazarus, MSW
Matthew Leary, PhD
Kay Loveland, PhD
Laurie Michaels, PhD
Don Murphy, PhD
Giuliana Reed, MSW
Ann Reifman, PhD
John Rhead, PhD
Murray Scher, PhD
Avrum Weiss, PhD
Sharilyn Wiskup, LPC

VOICES: THE ART AND SCIENCE OF PSYCHOTHERAPY (ISSN 0042-8272) is published by the American Academy of Psychotherapists, 230 Washington Ave Ext , Suite 101 / Albany, NY 12203.

Subscription prices for one year (three issues): $65 for individuals PDF only; $85 for individuals PDF & print copy; $249 for institutions. Orders by mail payable by check: 230 Washington Ave Ext, Suite 101 / Albany, NY 12203. Orders by MasterCard or Visa: call (518) 240-1178 or fax (518) 463-8656. Payments must be made in U.S. dollars through a U.S. bank made payable to *AAP Voices*. Some back volumes may be available from the *Voices* Business Office.

Change of Address: Please inform publisher as soon as a change to your email address is made. Send change of email address to aap@caphill.com.▼

Journal of the American Academy of Psychotherapists

VOICES

THE ART AND SCIENCE OF PSYCHOTHERAPY

Sometimes a catastrophe is only a course correction.

—James A. Owen

Journal of the American Academy of Psychotherapists

V O I C E S

THE ART AND SCIENCE OF PSYCHOTHERAPY

WTF?!? Oppression, Freedom and Self   Winter 2018: Volume 54, Number 3

WTF?!?

Reviews

Intervision

Poetry

Images

Calls for Papers

Voices

Cover Collage:
Ruins from Olympia
2018, Mary de Wit

©2018 by the American Academy of
Psychotherapists, Inc.
Published three times per year.
Cover Design: Mary de Wit
Design and Production by
Mary de Wit | in2Wit®, llc
AAP Web Site:
www.aapweb.com

Kristin Staroba

KRISTIN STAROBA, MSW, has a private practice in downtown Washington, DC, seeing adults in individual, couples, and group psychotherapy, and offering supervision. She has presented numerous times at AAP meetings and salons and is the Academy's president-elect.

kristin.staroba@gmail.com

Editorials

Next

THE FIRST EDITORIAL I WROTE FOR *VOICES*, IN THE SPRING ISSUE OF 2012, I CALLED "DANCING WITH *VOICES*." I spoke about my process of deciding to step up as editor, soft-shoeing from "Who, me? I'm hardly big enough," to putting on my slippers and sashaying to the middle of the floor. Realizing I could do this work was thrilling and terrifying; actually doing it has been deeply satisfying.

Six years and 18 issues later, I see the distance I've traveled personally and professionally. As I resurrected and refined my editorial chops, I grew more confident in the role and the work. I do edit well! I can find people to write! I do have something to say! Over the same span, I've freed up my own voice and loosened the binds that kept me small for a long time. I can generate referrals! I can speak plainly! I do want to show up!

In the course of this dance I've had many partners: co-editors Doris Jackson and Penelope Norton; the Editorial Review Board and the business team; numerous guest editors; many, many authors; the incoming editor, Carla Bauer; and, always, our graphic designer, Mary de Wit. To each I offer profound thanks.

Dancing has proven an apt metaphor for my AAP life. I was riveted by the experience of my first I&C Saturday night dance and joined before the next Summer Workshop. Every workshop seems to have rhythm and movement as we sway or twirl or boogie through it. As my tenure as editor was ending, I chose to run for Academy president and framed my candidate's statement as a dance with the Academy, recalling that first editorial.

This dance is done. On to the next! ▼

Carla Bauer

CARLA R. BAUER, LCSW, is in private practice in Atlanta, Georgia. A second career therapist, she brings over 25 years of corporate experience, as well as an earlier journey in theological studies, to her understanding of people and their struggles. Psychoanalytically trained, she seeks to blend psychodynamic and attachment orientations with a contemporary relational presence. When she can't be on the beach, the colors of the beach are on her! As incoming editor of *Voices*, she offers her voice to AAP.
crbauer01@bellsouth.net

Finding a Voice for Peaceful Discord

WHEN KRISTIN PROPOSED THE WTF?!? THEME, it resonated immediately with all of the bewilderment, frustration, and rage that simmer just below the surface (on a good day) as I watch events unfold in our political-social-cultural environment that seem determined to take us backward in the fights for freedom from oppression and self-actualization for all. I am amazed at how center stage politics have become in most of my circles, and even more amazed now when that doesn't seem to be so.

While politics were the backdrop of my childhood—growing up the child of a Louisiana politician and grandchild of an ardent opponent of the infamous Governor Huey Long—they rarely occupied any significant bandwidth in my own life. We were in the South, where the prevailing social contract was still a prohibition against talking about politics, religion, or sex. But lately, politics are everywhere—even in the therapy room, where my trauma clients come in seriously triggered by the actions of the president, others recount story after story of relationship conflict around political differences, and I, in turn, spend my own therapy time dealing with my political rage and conflicts. Now we talk about politics constantly, but civil discourse is increasingly rare.

I'm accustomed to living a life that crosses the political aisle. As a banker by prior career and a Democrat, I was always in the minority. And that was fine: Democrats and Republicans generally wanted the same things; our differences were mostly in beliefs about how best to achieve them, not particularly hard to tolerate. Besides, we never talked politics at work. I was typically in the minority at home as well, most of my family being much more conservative. But we didn't talk about it much there either. Again, it's the South. I might bristle quietly at my father's conservative stance, then go out and cancel his vote. One liberal sister, more vocal, is the lightning rod for whatever conflict does get aired. Siblings spar on Facebook, quickly spiraling into accusations of stupidity and epithets such as "libtard," making it clear that these are topics we can't discuss. In person, silence prevails, in the interest of peace. But it is a different silence now—one of knowing that we *cannot* talk of our political differences.

That silence and degeneration of discourse loom large for me. I struggle with what it means to gather for holidays with a family that can't even acknowledge our different views, much less talk about them. Or, even harder to grasp, what it means that some of my closest friends, "family of choice," can be on the other side of today's issues, of core values, conversation also off limits there. Now it seems to matter more that we don't—or can't—talk about politics, or the underlying values, or even about our intolerance of differences. It's not just about Democrat vs. Republican platforms anymore. There is so much more at stake.

Earlier this year, I saw *RBG*, a fabulous documentary about Ruth Bader Ginsburg, aka "The Notorius RBG" in pop culture. It's a movie that I recommend highly—and may she live long and healthy! One of the most moving parts of the film was the depiction of Ginsburg's deep friendship with fellow justice, Antonin Scalia. That these two people, for whom politics are front-and-center, at the very core of their lives, could come from opposite ends of the bench, where they sparred deeply over critical issues, yet remain close personal friends, is highly inspirational. If they could do it, surely we can. We must find ways to cross the aisle—as people and as therapists.

As much as the theme resonated, I struggled with how to write about it constructively and productively, not just rant. But authors in this issue found their voices and have written powerfully of their struggles to navigate our current political climate, to counter oppressive forces that interfere with self-fulfillment, and to sustain civil discourse in the face of political discord. Patti Digh kicks us off with her poignant account of raising a transgender child struggling to fulfill self-identity in a hostile environment. Phil Spiro describes the struggle to sustain civil discourse around political differences. Cherian Verghese gives us a rich exploration of how the historical narrative valorizing Whiteness shapes the experiences of people of color in this country; Samir Patel gives a moving commentary on his own experience with this narrative. Bonnie Buchele's difficulty in overcoming the overwhelm of traumatic political events to find something to say that would benefit her conference audience echoes the paralysis I find myself in, struggling to give constructive voice to my simmering political rage.

From our archives, we revisit Rhona Engels' prescient 2006 piece about the abiding American character of individualism, with new commentaries from Tom Burns and Dairlyn Chelette about its continued wisdom for today. Cathy Roberts shares experiences with the shame of "othering" and seeing microaggressions subtly creep into even dedicated support of diversity, while Lisa Kays questions what it means to be a White voice teaching diversity.

Susan McClure writes of the pain of being outcast for holding a moderate political position in an era of extremes. Nick Kirsch challenges us to look in the mirror and know that the abuses of power observed on the political scene occur in ourselves and our organizations as well. Polly Hart offers some resources for finding ways to talk about politics.

Beulah Amsterdam shares how a painful intergenerational trauma is retriggered by the present political environment. Lisa Kays and Gina Sangster write about how their own reactions to political issues seep into and impact their work with clients. Xanthia Johnson tells of a powerful new experience of being seen, after first experiencing an all too familiar invisibility as a person of color dealing with an American institution.

From the AAP tape library, Ernest Kramer's interview with Sidney Jourard includes the influence that Carl Whitaker, John Warkentin, and Tom Malone had on Jourard's orientation as a therapist and offers some insight into how aspects of the American culture are better understood by the historian than the compatriot. Elizabeth Field, Steven Ingram, and Scott Gilkeson tempt us into further reading with their rich book reviews. In Intervision, Bob Rosenblatt and respondents Barry Wepman, Rob Williams, and Nick Kirsch explore what makes a supervision group really click, and new poems by Jim Carpenter and Neal Whitman round out the issue.

This rich and timely issue is Kristin Staroba's final issue as editor, before she puts down her pen and picks up the mantle of AAP's president-elect. Please join me in thanking her for six years of excellent service to *Voices*! We are all made richer for it. And I have big shoes to fill.

Patti Digh

Raising Unicorns:
A Story of Radical Acceptance in an Inhospitable World

PATTI DIGH is the founder of The School of Inclusion + Activism, and author of eight books, including *Life is a Verb* and *The Geography of Loss*. *Life is a Verb* was one of five finalists for the prestigious Books for a Better Life Award when it was published. She is also the mom of two children who are her greatest teachers, one of whom is both Autistic and Transgender. Email her at *support@pattidigh.com*.

LAST SPRING, I WATCHED THE OLD MAN AS HE WATCHED FELIKS, MY THEN-14-YEAR-OLD SON, IN THE CEREAL AISLE AT HARRIS TEETER. And I knew in that instant what was coming next. "You a girl or a boy?" the old man asked. I waited where I was, half-facing the Cheerios—why are there so many varieties? I asked myself. And I waited to let Feliks handle this one on his own.

Feliks' eyes caught mine as he turned to look at the old man. "Pardon?" he said. "You a girl or a boy?" the old man asked again. Feliks looked him straight in the eye and slowly said, "Yes."

At the time, Feliks was sporting two sets of dangling earrings in each ear, a buzz cut that would have made Johnny Unitas proud, jeans, and a t-shirt that showed no obvious signs of girlhood because of the tight binder he has used every day for the past four years to lessen the appearance of breasts. He socially transitioned to his true identity as Feliks at 11, having lived the first 10 years of his life as a female assigned at birth.

One thing I should mention: We live in North Carolina, home to a legislature that has made world news for its regressive transgender policies, like its bathroom bill forcing transgender individuals to use the restroom that corresponds with the gender assigned to them at birth. Yes, *that* North Carolina is the context for this story.

This is the North Carolina in which I was called n-lover and spat on (and worse) by men in trucks with Confederate flags in 1977 as I walked with my African-American boyfriend near our college. This is the same North Carolina where the Greensboro Massacre took place in November 1979, blocks from our apartment, the KKK shooting people dead in the streets, the same North Carolina that opposed same-sex marriage, and the same North Carolina that voted for Trump. Otherness is a dangerous liability here—and sadly, in the nation.

Feliks' first forays into the world as Feliks were predictably male: button-up shirt with a necktie. Over time, he started waving his own flag, ranging from flowered pants to jeans, from iridescent makeup to bowties, from skinny jeans and fluffy tops with smiley faces, to combat boots and camo. If you approached the situation with a false sense of binary—male or female—you were bound to misread or even worry that you couldn't pinpoint which he was, and that false binary is often hard to overcome, because it is so ingrained.

When our daughter, Emma, had joined the middle school band years before, I was caught short by my own unspoken belief that girls don't play the trombone and tuba. Well, they didn't in my day. She disabused me of that belief by carrying a heavy sousaphone while marching at football games through high school and college, for eight years of kickoffs and homecomings. It was a belief I didn't even know I had until I was face-to-face with it. Perhaps we don't know what we believe until the opposite is presented to us.

And now this: A girl transitioning into the boy he was meant to be, his real identity, in a political and social environment that would likely do nothing less than chew him up and spit him out.

As this process unfolded, I recalled a pirate birthday party we had held for Feliks when he was turning six, still living as a girl. Parties were hard on him. The noise, the unexpected, the social interaction—all of it. In the dining room, in a rare quiet moment amidst the treasure hunt, this girl I had given birth to turned to me, very seriously looked me in the eye, and said, "I'm a boy, you know" and sped away to join the pirates in the front yard.

Perhaps I shouldn't have discounted that. Perhaps I should have listened more deeply. Perhaps I should have really heard him in that moment, but the pirates in the front yard were screaming for more pirate ship cake, and the party swirled on around us, as did life.

Since his transition to living as Feliks, these "are you a girl or a boy" kinds of encounters happen with some regularity as we make our way through our days. "What would you girls like to eat?" we are asked in restaurants. "Thanks, ladies," from clerks in stores. None of it seems to faze Feliks, one advantage to being Autistic in addition to transgender: He doesn't care what other people think of him, and when I ask if I should correct people in the moment, he says, "It really doesn't matter to me."

He was a difficult child—a screamer. One afternoon after hours of screaming, I felt I might hurt him if we didn't leave the house, so I drove to the Tops Shoe store in Asheville, parked the car, got him out of his car seat, and walked in the door closest to the children's shoe department. The woman who had helped us with Emma's shoes for years took one look at me and simply held out her arms. I handed him over and sat in the women's department for a long time while she held Feliks and comforted him while fitting children for shoes.

We didn't know until his diagnosis at age nine that he was Autistic. He has high-functioning Autism or Asperger's Syndrome, as it used to be called. We told him the findings of the long diagnostic process one summer evening on the front porch, in green rocking chairs, as the sun set. We presented it as a different "operating system," like a PC and a Mac have different operating systems, both of which work well, but sometimes have trouble communicating between them.

We gave him a book of famous people with Asperger's or who were believed to have had Asperger's, including his hero, Einstein, which lit him up. "I have superpowers!" he said. That evening he created a bumper sticker that is still on the back of our car: "I'm an Aspie, and I'm proud of it!" it reads.

That fall, his teacher told us when she introduced a new child in the classroom who had diabetes and explained what that meant and how the other kids could help her, Feliks stood up next, proudly announced he had Asperger's, and explained what that meant and how the other kids could help *him*.

Being diagnosed was a relief for Feliks: "*this* is *why* I am the way I am," he understood. "I am not broken; I just have a different operating system." Had we presented it in a different way or been too ashamed to even tell him, as are some parents, how different his life with Autism would be. He would be invested in brokenness. Instead, he has superpowers.

Before that diagnosis, we were in despair—and still are now, sometimes, even often. We are often moving forward into new, alien, inhospitable territory without a map, as is Feliks—and the territory is getting more inhospitable by the day.

Feliks could hold it together at school but would start raging in the car on the way home, a meltdown that could last for hours, and often did. "Help me, help me, help me," he would scream; we waited for the police to arrive many days, knowing how easy it would be for a passerby to become alarmed and call the authorities. Which they did once, when I was alone and trying to extricate him from a birthday party that caused a meltdown disruptive to the other partygoers. As I struggled to carry him to the car, legs and arms hitting me while he screamed until I thought my eardrum was punctured, I could see people on the balcony above the parking lot watching; someone called the police, thinking I was kidnapping him.

Because of a bullying situation at school directed at Feliks' autism, one the school seemed incapable of handling, we took him out of elementary school and "unschooled" him for three years—the hardest three years of my life. We were deep into puberty which can be traumatic for any kid, much less a transgender one, and everything was exaggerated—the moods, the oppositional behavior, the 5 hour meltdowns. Every day felt like walking in a minefield, with no discernable pattern as to where the mines were placed.

As we sat in the living room one night, each typing on our laptops ten feet away from each other, I got a message from Feliks with a video about a young transgender man and his journey from assigned female at birth to male.

I wrote back, a form of communication we use often with Feliks, for whom spoken conversation is sometimes too confronting and difficult to process. "This is interesting. I have a lot of transgender friends, so I appreciate your sending it to me. But I'm wondering why you sent it."

I got this message in response: "Because that's me."

That was his coming out statement, one I was surprised by, I'll admit, but I saw my job, our job, as being supportive. That does not mean I didn't have doubts or even secretly wish that things wouldn't get harder for him than they already were.

Before coming out to us, Feliks would only appear in public in a full-body costume, each covering his whole body, including his head. We didn't yet know why this was true, but when we realized these costumes were the only thing that made it possible for him to interact in the world, we bought the one of his dreams: Cynder.

Cynder is a professional looking "mascot" furry, a bright yellow fox that covered him from head to toe, and made him somewhat of a local celebrity. We would venture into Harris Teeter for brownie mix, and Cynder would be beset with requests for selfies, while as himself he simply could not be seen. All that changed when he transitioned to become Feliks. He was able to go into the world as himself then. The physical disconnect was gone when he showed up as his true self, though the Autism remained. It is remarkable what can happen when you fully become who you are, I learned.

But in the summer of 2015, our life hit its nadir. Feliks was staying up all night and sleeping during the day, scaring us with his manic behavior. And then I found the medications that had made life bearable—Prozac and Risperdal: He was stockpiling them rather than taking them. And would take them no more, short of physical violence to get him to swallow them, which we also tried, in desperation. But in a quiet moment, I knew he was better able to tell what he needed than I was, and that there must be some reason he was no longer taking the pills, just as he had discovered he could go out in public in a costume. We didn't need him to explain it. It wasn't easy to come to that conclusion about the medication, given the consequences.

I stayed up all night with him for months, afraid he would hurt himself or run out the front door into the lake. Only then would I sleep, between 7:00 and 8:00 a.m., getting up then for another day of work. I was so exhausted, both mentally and physically, that I started hallucinating. I told my husband that I could not do it any longer. I held an annual event that September and sobbed each time I got up to the microphone. I was broken in two, eating Tums like candy because of "heartburn," unaware that the left anterior descending artery of my heart was 95% blocked. I had my first heart attack a few months later.

What have I learned in this journey into Autism and the transgender community in a world in which the president of the United States mocks people with disabilities and bans people who are transgender? It can be distilled into two, perhaps unlikely, statements: *Allow people to surprise you* and *love without needing to understand first*.

One evening in 2016, after literally spending six months in bed, Feliks sat up and told his dad it was time for him to go back to school. "Well, I can't very well spend the rest of my life in bed, now can I?" he said, sweeping his hand around the room. Surprised, we tried to find a middle school that might accept this Autistic, transgender child. As we drove through cow fields to get to one school on our list, I despaired at finding acceptance there. But when we arrived, the principal had prepared for our meeting with a gender plan printed and ready for us to fill out together.

Two years later, an ROTC captain would respond with similar grace when Feliks asked about joining the ROTC in high school: "Well, while this presents some support requirements we haven't dealt with before, our goal is to help every student be successful." Did I think an ROTC captain would have the grace to talk about "support requirements" instead of responding from a more subjective space? I'll admit, I did not. He surprised me. And I allowed him to surprise me.

That middle school amidst cow fields was the best two years of Feliks' life—and of ours. "Like night and day," everyone said. In his own time, he had done internally what he needed to do, and could show up fully as himself, hair dyed a different color every month, Napoleon Dynamite glasses, and all. The kids and the school accepted him as he was, even if that presentation changed day-to-day, which it frequently did.

He had friends for the first time in his life, a cadre of seven girls who liked his company and enjoyed his humor, invited him to sleepovers, only one of which was interrupted by a transphobic parent. He took horseback riding lessons twice a week, gaining strength and confidence. He tried out for the soccer team. He ran for president of the Beta Club. He was on the A/B Honor Roll every quarter.

You can imagine how happy we were for him. And for us—this all translated into fewer meltdowns, more mature responses, and a happier home. We had a life again. It wouldn't last.

What about my own journey?

In May of 2015, I had started seeing a psychiatrist for the first time. I was 55 years old. His shoes were almost always brown. Sometimes his socks matched his bright green jacket, which I think was worn on days with rain. But I can't be sure; my evidence is sketchy, inconsistent, and random. I sat across from him, on a nubby burnt orange sofa that felt sturdy and newish and was so dark it was almost red; it was long enough for a family of four, depending on the capacity of that family for closeness. Which, perhaps, was the point in his line of work.

I was convinced I was clinically depressed, because getting dressed had become almost impossible and showering was impossible, because hiding was the story of most days, and because my family doctor had no solutions, seemingly, except to cut short the conversations when I said the word, "depressed," and double the prescription of Celexa, which wasn't helping and still wouldn't help at twice the dose.

And so, I found myself in an office with a psychiatrist across the room from me in those brown shoes and green socks, a mantle slightly above and to the left of his head, covered in knick-knacks with great meaning, I'm sure, that sturdy burnt orange couch my perch, constant traffic outside the window as an aside.

Ninety minutes later, after a flood of talk that overflowed the banks of that particular river and into the next person's appointment, I emerged *without* Celexa and with a diagnosis not of depression but of PTSD.

I laughed when he said those four letters, adding after the laugh, "Well, that's ridiculous." I thought he was joking.

"PTSD? That's for soldiers and survivors of violence," I added, trying to cover up my laugh when I realized he was serious.

And then he cocked his head to one side, raised one eyebrow, and recounted the events of the last four years back to me: "Significant betrayal and slander by one of your closest friends and business partners after 8 years (and rejection by all those who believed his slander), brother's heart attack and quintuple bypass surgery, Autism diagnosis for your child, cancer diagnosis for your husband, transgender transition for your child, daughter leaving for college, graduating from college, traveling the world alone, getting a job, finding an apartment, a friend's attempted suicide, and then her completed one, death of your best friend and several pets you've had for twenty years, significant financial losses because of a new business partner who lied about his capabilities, a move to a new town, in part because of those losses, mother's decline, dementia and death. In four years."

The list went on from there even. It went on. And now I could add to it: Heart attack. Stent. Heart attack. Stent.

I listened, and then deflected: "Yeah, but that's just life," I said. "Everybody deals with things like that all the time. That's what life is."

Slowly he reiterated his diagnosis, and outlined his proposed treatment plan.

I thought to myself:

When you are the person who endures, it comes as a shock when you simply cannot any longer, when showering and dressing and thinking have become too much. When cooking is out of the question. Or even eating.

When you are the person who holds it together for everyone else, it comes as a shock when you start unraveling, unable to help even yourself.

What would I tell a friend who recounted that list to me? I would say, "Dear sweet little baby Jesus, take a break. Rest, catch your breath, do some serious self-care, get some help, you are home to a life."

What had I been telling myself? "Buck up, this is life. Everybody is dealing with the same kinds of things, many a lot worse than this. You've got work to do. Don't ask for help, just put your head down and run at it. That has always worked."

I wrote four books in those four years. I honestly have no idea how I did that. I traveled. I spoke. I saw my husband and children through illness and transitions of many kinds. I survived two business partners who shattered my sense of who I am. I carried on.

We carry on.

We carry on, don't we?

We carry on with things significant and insignificant.

We are the competent ones. We are the ones who carry on, who become stoic instead of hysterical, the ones who shoulder a weight like it is nothing, nothing at all. We are the ones who make it right for everyone, who don't say no if you need help, but almost always say no to ourselves.

When wealthy white male privilege seats an unqualified, racist, sexist, Islamophobic, ableist president and a deeply unqualified judge on the Supreme Court, we carry on. When our children's lives are disrespected and in danger just because of who they are, we simply up our game. We say, as Pat Schroeder used to, that "you can't wring your hands and roll up your sleeves at the same time." We carry on. Until we can't any longer.

When I was a child, my father used to involve us in the chores, one of which was scrubbing the white wall tires on our car with bleach and a toothbrush every week. He would say to me and my brother, "If you want something done right, do it yourself." And evidently I believed him, taking everything on, even things no one had asked me to take on.

As I investigated this new diagnosis, I saw that the incidence of PTSD among mothers whose children have Autism is very high, higher than combat soldiers. And I understand that now; the days are full of old and new mines that will explode at a time I cannot know. I cannot know where to step to avoid the explosions. Add everything else on my list, and I now have no trouble at all believing that diagnosis.

I sat on that couch once a month for almost two years, driving an hour each way to get there. And truths were revealed to me, most often in my own processing, as words fell from my mouth onto a lovely Persian rug that clashed, but beautifully, with his chair. What I thought, I can no longer think. What I did to help people, I can no longer do. Because now I can see boundaries being crafted like one stitches a beloved doll's head back on her old body after too much love and wear. Stitches to hold me together, to not let me ooze into the other, articulating for myself what "I have to" means. It really means, "I am choosing to." I am choosing to kill myself slowly by being a sleep-deprived, stressed-out mother of an Autistic, transgender child, who more than anything, needs me to stay alive.

I sit on a different couch now, in a different town, facing a different man who never wears brown shoes, always black. We sit there twice a month, doing acceptance and behavior therapy, an approach that appeals to the "buck up, cupcake" side of my personality and has also shown in living color the "away moves" I make relative to what and whom I say I value most. They are writ large over my lifetime and some have persisted until today: overeating, procrastination, drinking, drugs, and the list goes on. It appears I am something of a professional at moving away instead of toward. Perhaps it comes with persistently being in survival mode.

Feliks rarely goes outside now. Again. It feels as if we have regressed to those hard years before middle school. The transition to high school was too much for Feliks. He attended one day and couldn't go back. "Why?" I asked, not remembering that "why" is often more a challenge than a question. "I DON'T KNOW," he screamed. "I DON'T KNOW." We'll have to live with not knowing then.

He is in a liminal space at 15: having to wait until 16 to take the GED, start hormone therapy, and take community college classes. What about the next 8 months? So far, we are back in the old patterns of obstinance, sleeping all day and up all night, and raging. Imagine how hard this is for him.

It was so good for those two years. It wasn't without its challenges, but there was sunlight. And now it feels like nighttime again.

I know life is not a straight line. But I had let hope take precedence and was blindsided by this regression. Or is it a regression? Perhaps this is the path forward, as much as it feels like we are dancing backward at a rapid pace. This is true of my family's experience, and it is true of our nation's experience, where we are all in survival mode, and it is taking its toll. And upping our game, simply carrying on, has real consequences.

Through all of this, through all the "othering" and rejection of difference, my wish is that every child—every person—feel this:

Raising Unicorns: A Story of Radical Acceptance 11

Whatever you need, we will open space for you to get it, even if we don't understand it.
Whatever you say, we will believe you, even if we don't understand it.
Whatever you do, we will love you, even if we don't understand it.
Whomever you love, we will support you, even if we don't understand it.

Because having to understand first often precludes love. It stops us.

And in the meantime, we sit, and we talk; we recognize, and we stitch ourselves back together again. ▼

Philip Spiro

PHILIP SPIRO, MD, received his
medical degree from Yale and
ultimately trained in psychiatry
at Duke, after brief flirtation with
training in surgery and two years
of general medical practice in rural
North Carolina. He has practiced
psychiatry in Chapel Hill, North
Carolina since 1990. In addition to
his clinical practice, he is also on the
teaching faculty at Duke Medical
Center and is involved in the training and supervision of psychiatric
residents.
Philip.Spiro@duke.edu

I'm Right, You're Wrong…
How's That Working for You?

A FEW YEARS AGO, I HAD A CONVERSATION WITH
A FRIEND. Though, as I write, it seems more appropriate to call it what it was—a mean-spirited argument with this guy I know. I'll call him Paul. He isn't
a patient, so I don't have to protect confidentiality, and
he isn't likely to read *Voices*, so I don't have to protect
his feelings. I just need some distance. So I'll write about
"Paul" and not use his real name. He'd recognize himself, though he would, I am sure, tell this story in a very
different way.

What were we arguing about? Honestly, I can't remember. We differ on so many subjects, and we'd had
many so-called "discussions." It could have been about
anything: abortion, the war in Iraq, racism, taxes, the
death penalty, assisted suicide, or frankly whether the
sky was blue. I really don't remember, and it doesn't really
matter. What I do remember is that this particular argument, I'm going to say it was about Obamacare, was more
heated, more irritating, and more dispiriting to both of
us than we had thus far experienced. We had started our
conversation, as we always attempted to do, as two reasonable men—"let us sit down and reason together"—
trying to talk about an issue near and dear to both of our
hearts. We were both passionate, and we each had deeply
personal reasons to be so. I am in medicine and see, just
about every day, the direct personal effect of our broken
healthcare system. Paul had recently had some medical
problems and was very happy with how the medical system had worked for him. We were both convinced that
we were right and that the other was wrong. And we were
both convinced it was vitally important to get the other
person to change his view.

However, despite our good intentions, this "reason" thing did not happen. The discussion went rapidly downhill. Passion overcame reason. It got loud. It got irritating. And it got mean, very mean. Being a generally civil person, I would love to say we didn't descend to name calling. But we did. I'm quite sure it was all in "fun." Of course. I do remember he called me a "commie libtard" [insert steamed-face emoji here], and I do believe I called him a "fascist" [insert shame-faced emoji here]. Though we generally worked well together, this conversation was clearly going south really quickly.

We were in a vicious cycle and each time we went back and forth it got louder, more personal, and more ad hominem. I felt like he was calling me stupid. No, it was more than "felt like." He was actually doing it—he was openly telling me that I didn't have the intelligence to comprehend the problem accurately. He was calling me mean, accusing me of trying to hurt people, "like all you liberals," by making them dependent. And he was calling me lazy—he actually used that word—declaring that I was too weak-willed to delve, as he had done, into the real facts of the matter, and that if I would just do that, I would agree with him.

Not surprisingly, this argument didn't end well. We both stormed off convinced that the other person was a moron. And, though it would make a great story, we have never really recovered. We work together, so we have learned to be civil with each other. But we've learned to avoid talking about politics, religion, and just about everything else other than the task at hand. Even talking about the weather seems risky.

I try not to comment on the Trump sticker on his pickup truck, and he doesn't comment on the Obama sticker on my Prius.

You are familiar with this kind of story—unless you live in a bubble, or a hole, or a silo, or a bunker. Or never go to Thanksgiving dinner. Or never watch TV. In these (dare I say, dark) days, my story is not unusual. Patients and colleagues in my office talk about relationships fractured over politics. People seem to make extraordinary efforts to avoid talking with anyone who might disagree with them about any controversial topic, lest the conversation explode. Worse, people avoid even hearing a non-conforming opinion. I recently suggested to a friend that she listen to a conservative talk radio program just so she could get a sense of "the other side." Her reply (verbatim, because it literally happened just yesterday) was, "I don't care what they think—they're all a bunch of stupid idiots." This comment from an otherwise reasonable person.

Three things came my way around the same time as my argument with Paul, each having a profound effect. No, they did not make it all better. No, they did not turn Paul into a liberal. No, they did not lead to Paul and me walking off into the sunset together singing "Imagine" (or "America the Beautiful," as he would have it). But they did change how I look at our schismatic culture and how I have been surviving in this world since November 9, 2016.

The first was a patient. A young man with whom I had been working for a few months, a college student at one of our local notoriously liberal universities, was telling me with some evident hesitation—he accurately sensed my political leanings and knows I drive a Prius—that he had voted for Romney. He was breaching the firewall: "This is therapy, let's not talk about politics—unless, of course, we agree." He was doing so because he trusted me and because he was in pain. He felt painfully estranged and isolated from his liberal classmates who were openly mocking him. They could not believe that someone so close at hand—someone in their "in-group"—was so stupid as to vote for Romney, or so mean as to advocate conservative policies which hurt people, or so lazy as to have not read any Marxist critique of capitalism. Stupid. Mean. Lazy. Yet he was objectively none of those things. He was an intelligent, compassionate, hard-working, and open-minded young man, who happened to hold conservative political views. But here's the light bulb moment: As he was telling his story, I found myself personally resonating with his distress. My altercation with Paul was recent and it was not hard to remember how I felt. The political poles were reversed—he was the conservative and his friends were the liberals—yet he and I felt the same way. This wasn't a conservative/liberal thing. This was a "how you think about someone who disagrees with you" thing: how it feels to be thought of as deficient just because you disagree, and how easy it is to dehumanize the other by labeling them as unintelligent, mean-spirited, or lazy.

Hearing this college student, who was so hurt that he was hesitant to tell even his therapist about his political leanings, made me look back on my argument with Paul. It was important. And embarrassing. I was hurt when he called me stupid, mean, and lazy. But, to be completely honest, I had been doing the very same thing to him. Maybe not as overtly—I tend to keep my knives hidden—but I was doing it nonetheless. Covertly, implicitly, and with gussied-up four syllable words, but it was there. And whether I was saying it or not, I was certainly thinking it. I'm not very good at keeping my opinion hidden, and I'm sure that it was leaking out my pores. No wonder our argument had gone badly. Who wants to debate someone about facts when the conversation turns so quickly to character?

So, can I proceed forward and try not to do that again? I'm trying. Over the last two years my resolve has been tested. Confession: I listen to conservative talk radio, Rush Limbaugh and Sean Hannity to be precise. On occasion, OK? Just to learn, OK? I feel defensive even acknowledging this publicly to what I assume to be the generally liberal readership of this journal. On their programs, I hear talk about people like me. Liberals and others on my side of the political spectrum are routinely called these exact same words—stupid, mean, and lazy. They don't even try to cover it up. They just come flat out and say it. I actually admire that kind of directness. At the same time, I hear the anger on the other side of the spectrum. Limbaugh and Hannity always seem to be so damn angry. As do their listeners. Why is that? And in moments of weakness I am tempted to label them as mentally ill—doesn't such underlying anger point to something psychologically amiss? Yet as I listen more carefully, I hear the hurt that drives the anger. Limbaugh, Hannity, and those they shout for, have been feeling like I (we) have been doing the same thing to them—calling them stupid, mean, and lazy—for years. They are fed up. And, I've got to say, they're right. I've done it; I've heard others do it since I was a child growing up in a progressive bubble.

So, who started this mess? Wouldn't it be their job to stop it? Those on the left tell me it was started by those on the right. Those on the right tell me it was started by those on the left. I submit it doesn't matter. If you're in a stand-off, someone has to risk putting their gun down. Starting to consider that your political opponents are smart, well intended, and diligent is a really good way to start.

Back to Paul. The second thing that happened around my argument with Paul was an article I came across about effective argumentation. The authors were cognitive neuroscientists who were researching the most productive ways to debate difficult topics (Fisher, Knobe, Strickland, and Keil, 2018). Specifically, they posit, and this is no huge paradigm shift for therapists, that there are two basic strategies which they call "arguing to win" and "arguing to learn." Using experimental protocols, they seek to understand which strategy fosters more effective dialogue and which helps people come up with better solutions. So again, particularly for therapists, there is no earth-shattering revelation. If you are trying to come up with mutually acceptable solutions arguing to win doesn't work so well. It quickly drives people into hyperpolarized black/white positions and inhibits further dialogue. So, if you are interested in that outcome, by all means, argue to win. You will lose, even if you win. If, however, you are trying to find common ground, arguing to learn works a lot better. Again, we therapists know this. Ask any marital therapist. Seeking to understand someone creates the open space in which people can find solutions. May I suggest we approach our political opponents with curiosity not judgment? But we, and I do not exclude myself from this, seem to be wired to win as well as wired to get along. The former is easy and, in my opinion, our default mode. The latter takes work. Again, this is no huge discovery. I know it and knew it already. But having the words to put to it helps me when I encounter political difference. I realize, in retrospect, that both Paul and I had been arguing to win, and it didn't go so well.

The third thing that crossed my path about this same time was *moral foundations theory* as outlined in Jonathan Haidt's book *The Righteous Mind* (2012). Moral foundations theory posits that we make our moral choices based upon one or more of six moral foundations. Analogizing that these foundations are like "taste receptors," Haidt argues that each person has them—all six—in ways that are hard-wired into our brains. Human beings differ in how strongly each is wired as well as how we have been culturally programmed to value one foundation more than another. When we attempt to decide whether an action is right or wrong we consult our six moral foundations, which are: Care/Harm, Fairness/Cheating, Liberty/Oppression, Loyalty/Betrayal, Authority/Subversion and Purity/Degradation. An action is deemed right or wrong based upon whether it does someone harm, whether it is fair, whether it impinges on someone's liberty, whether it betrays one's group, whether it subverts an authority, or whether it is pure. Space precludes a full explanation of the theory, but Haidt proposes (and this is supported by his research) that liberals and conservatives differ on which moral foundations they tend to use. Those on the liberal end of the political spectrum tend to make moral decisions based upon the first three foundations. It is morally permissible to do something, no matter how unusual or strange, if it does not hurt anyone (the Care/Harm foundation), if the playing field is even (the Fairness/Cheating foundation), and if it does not oppress anyone (the Liberty/Oppression foundation). Those on the conservative end of the spectrum use these three foundations as well, but also factor in the other three, which liberals tend to downplay, ignore, or dismiss. To a conservative, an action might be morally wrong, even if it doesn't harm someone, because it betrays one's group (the Loyalty/Betrayal foundation), because it subverts authority (the Authority/Subversion foundation), or because it is impure (the Purity/Degradation foundation).

As far as my argument with Paul is concerned, what I gleaned from Moral Foundations Theory was that Paul isn't really stupid, mean, or lazy—I know, in my more considerate mind, that he is none of these—he just bases his political conclusions on a very different moral base than I do. I am a classic liberal. As far as I am concerned, if it doesn't hurt anyone else, feel free to do it. Paul is clearly more conservative in his moral foundations. He values loyalty, authority, and sanctity much more than I do. He's much more of a classic "patriot" than I am. That's the loyalty/betrayal foundation. He has an American flag on his truck and resonates positively with the phrase "my country right or wrong." He's the one chanting "USA, USA, USA" in a crowd. He's much more of a rule follower than I am. That's the authority/subversion foundation. Rules should be followed even if you disagree with them, even if violating them doesn't hurt anyone, and even if you won't get caught. And he's clearly more religious than I am. That's the purity/degradation foundation. He attends a conservative church and is inclined to think some things should be kept sacred even if I don't think it matters, even if you do it in private. His political opinions flow directly from his values. And this explains, without judgment, our radical differences in that arena.

Again, this is a story still being written. There is no fairy-tale ending. Frankly I doubt there will be. Détente may be the best Paul and I can get to. But I hope for more. It's that important. Paul and I still have a connection, we do some work together, so there is still hope. But there is a chasm between us. And so many culturally sanctioned ways to reinforce our separate silos and stay apart. From what I can tell, Paul doesn't even want to bridge the divide. But I have become personally committed, with this Paul and future Paul's, to try to fight this tendency to make myself feel better by labeling my opponent as stupid, mean, or lazy. To try to understand, not persuade, when I encounter someone who disagrees with me—to argue to learn, not argue to win. And to try to grasp that other people's values are as compelling to them as mine are to me, even if I don't understand them at all or if the policy positions these values lead them to is beyond my immediate comprehension.

Maybe all is not lost. Paul and I did come up with a place to start. We agreed that before we started talking about anything of contention, he would say one good thing about Obama and I would say one good thing about Trump. We haven't had a chance to try this yet, but it did work with a patient, an older gentleman whom I have seen for over twenty years. We meet every few months for medication management at this point, but it's been clear for a long time that we are, shall we say, of radically different political stripe. Generally, and appropriately, we tend to avoid that subject, which might be too contentious to address. But, knowing he had voted for Trump and knowing he would be hesitant to bring that up with me (he knows I drive the aforementioned Prius after all), I casually mentioned during one of our sessions—it wasn't out of context and it was indeed genuine—that I thought Trump had handled something reasonably well. My patient didn't immediately join in with me to offer similar praise for Obama. That would be too much to hope for. But he did smile, genuinely. And the rest of our meeting went surprisingly warmly. It seemed to work. So, I am looking forward to trying this out with Paul. ▼

References:

Fisher, M., Knobe, J., Strickland, B., & Keil, F. (2018, February). The tribalism of truth, *Scientific American, 318.*

Haidt, J. (2012). *The righteous mind: Why good people are divided by politics and religion.* New York: Pantheon Books.

Cherian Verghese

Race, Melancholia,
and the Fantasy of Whiteness

Until the story of the hunt is told by the lion, the tale of the hunt will always glorify the hunter.
— Ewe mina saying

CHERIAN VERGHESE, PHD, is a psychologist in private practice since 1990 in Washington, DC. He provides individual and couple psychotherapy as well as individual and group supervision. A faculty member of the Washington School of Psychiatry and a founding and steering committee member of its Center for the Study of Race, Ethnicity and Culture, Cherian is also faculty at the Institute for Contemporary Psychotherapy and Psychoanalysis. In 2002, he founded the South Asian Mental Health Association. Cherian is a native of Kerala, South India. He was married to a White American woman and raised a bi-cultural child. He is most excited now with playing grandfather to his first grandchild.
cverghese@mindspring.com

I

CRITICAL PEDAGOGY TEACHES US THAT OUR KNOWLEDGE OF WHO WE ARE—AND HAVE BEEN—AS A NATION IS PROFOUNDLY INFLUENCED BY THE SPECIFIC NARRATIVES SURROUNDING OUR COLLECTIVE HISTORY. Such historical narratives enshrine a view of American history that valorizes a decidedly White male perspective, where women and people of color exist mostly as supporting casts or are entirely absent, erased. Inculcated in us during our formative years, these narratives are continually repeated and reaffirmed through various social, educational, religious, and mass media exposures. These narratives impact our lives, patients' and therapists', and they do so differentially, depending on our individual situatedness, racially, culturally, nationally, and historically.

II

In his book *Truth and Method* (1960/1989), philosophical hermeneutist Hans Georg Gadamer states,

> ... [H]istory does not belong to us; we belong to it. Long before we understand ourselves through the process of self-examination, we understand ourselves in a self-evident way in the family, society, and state in which we live. The focus of subjectivity is a distorting mirror. The self-awareness of the individual is only a flickering in the closed

circuits of historical life. *That is why the prejudices of the individual, far more than his judgements, constitute the historical reality of his being* (pp. 276-277).

Gadamer's notion of prejudice encompasses all the ways in which our perception of ourselves and our world is inevitably colored by our unique lived experiences within the contexts of our culture and history. What thus appear as self-evident truths, including our understanding of ourselves and the world in which we live, often remain as implicit associations, even unconscious, while they profoundly influence how we see and interact with ourselves, others, and the world at large.

The hermeneutic perspective suggests that to engage in "true conversations," we need to first recognize our inevitable prejudices and the worldviews they form and, at least momentarily, step outside of those, into the unknown, to allow the truth of the other to inform us, even influence us. (That is consistent, to a degree, with Bion's [1967] recommendation to psychotherapists that they approach each session "without memory or desire"). True conversations have the potential for transforming both partners. Unfortunately, there are significant challenges arrayed against meeting the hermeneutic requirement, especially when society selectively rewards and punishes us for knowing and/or acting on our knowing of the deeper truths about ourselves, our fellow humans, and our embedding cultural surround including our true history. That process of social construction of our reality was central to Paulo Freire's (1968/1970) paradigm shifting observations on the oppressive nature of his Native Brazilian educational system, a commentary as well on the destructive, dehumanizing impact of colonization. Criticizing the method of education where the teacher "deposits" knowledge into the student, one that privileges the colonizer group, as the "banking method," Freire proposed that education should be a consciously engaged and mutually influencing process which has the potential for transforming the individual and society. He coined the term "conscientization" for such dialogic education.

Bringing this a bit closer to where we live as psychotherapists, it should be clear that such a process afflicts our own profession in a profound manner; it has been addressed by a number of analysts/therapists. They include the early and pioneering work of Frantz Fanon (1967), the revolutionary French colonial writer/psychiatrist from Martinique, and other, more recent, authors (Gump, 2010; Suchet, 2007; Holmes, 2006; Jones and Obourn, 2014; Leary, 2006). The video "Black Psychoanalysts Speak" (Winograd, 2014) provides us a window into the process of racism and its pernicious effects on the membership of our organizations, calling for a recognition of the actual lived experiences of African Americans and members of other oppressed groups, in our racialized country as well as within psychoanalytic organizations. Given the cultural and racial context of virulent anti-Semitism during the birthing of psychoanalysis, and the real threats to the survival of its Jewish founder Sigmund Freud and his earliest followers, it isn't surprising that the theory became one of the intrapsychic, to be managed within the unitary mind. Gillman (1993) writing on that topic suggested that Freud likely projected his own sense of Jewish inferiority onto women, thus seeing them as deficient, and emphasized castration anxiety. Only much later, in fits and starts, did psychoanalysis open up to the reality of the outer world, which includes considerable dangers, especially to various marginalized populations.

What continues to be poorly recognized is the impact of racialized processes on

White Americans, therapists, and patients, as they have not been encouraged to look at themselves and the roles they play, not always consciously, in maintaining the status quo and inadvertently continuing the oppression, a process that impoverishes us all. Robin DiAngelo (2011) tackles a challenge I have often faced (of course, I bring my own anxiety and prejudices to this as well) when working with White therapists on issues of race, in a provocative article in the International Journal of Critical Pedagogy titled "White Fragility." She states,

> White people in North America live in a social environment that protects and insulates them from race-based stress. This insulated environment of racial protection builds white expectations for racial comfort while at the same time lowering the ability to tolerate racial stress, leading to what I refer to as White Fragility. White Fragility is a state in which even a minimum amount of racial stress becomes intolerable, triggering a range of defensive moves. These moves include the outward display of emotions such as anger, fear, and guilt, and behaviors such as argumentation, silence, and leaving the stress-inducing situation. These behaviors, in turn, function to reinstate white racial equilibrium (pp. 54-70).

A "privileged White girl" patient of mine, June, who would turn a shade paler at any observations about our differences, shared with me her distress when an African American colleague hinted that she was abusing her privilege. She excused herself to "run to the bathroom and have a good cry" before she could return to work. Her use of PWG as a way of collapsing any talk of race or culture with me was the way she "ran to the bathroom to cry," as that talk brought up a level of discomfort she typically hasn't had to deal with, a privilege most people of color, including her therapist, do not possess. It was meaningful when she became truly concerned for my safety during the aftermath of the elections, a sign of her acknowledgement of our different situatedness within our increasingly racialized and polarized national environment. She was then also able to bring up her fear that, despite any outward indications from my side, any of her problems must seem insignificant to me, a dark-skinned immigrant who must have to deal with so much more injustices. This allowed further exploration of our various differences and their meaning and influence on our intersubjective experiences with each other, including male-female, White-not White, native-immigrant, and others.

III

In February of 2016, the Washington School of Psychiatry's Center for the Study of Race, Ethnicity and Culture organized a conference around Howard University Professor Clarence Lusane's presentation, "What the Elections Mean for Race Relations in America." (This article was originally presented on a panel at that conference, in a truncated form.) Lusane, author of *The Black History of the White House* (2010), identified four stages of racism in the United States: slavery, Jim Crow, voting rights, and our current post-Obama presidency. He then identified the profound backsliding that followed each of the major gains people of color attained using strategic dog-whistle code speak such as "law and order," "take America back," and "States' rights." For example, Lusane said, after the Emancipation Proclamation, which outlawed slave labor that had been the backbone of the South's economy, a compromise was offered in the convict labor exception, which allowed for the use of incarcerated individuals as free or near-free labor; this resulted in a dramatic increase in the number of Blacks, especially men, who were incarcerated, thus offsetting some of the loss through abolition of slavery. An often not recognized sequela of incarceration is that it disempowers a significant portion of marginalized populations, especially young Black men, by taking away their hard-won voting rights, which are denied to felons, making it nearly impossible for them to find meaningful work and to develop/maintain functional and vitally-needed human connections and families. Such insidious socio-political machinations help perpetuate the negative stereotypes of Black men and maintain the illusion of superiority of the White race.

Our nation's idealized, i.e., "White"-washed, history has allowed, perhaps even required, a revisionist notion of American Exceptionalism. That concept originally referred to the then-unique form of governance established at the founding of this nation with checks and balances in power provided by the three branches of the U.S. government, contrasting it to European nations where power was concentrated in an individual ruler or a group of ruling elites. American Exceptionalism has more recently come to mean something like "we/Americans are better than anyone else." And, in the current Trumpian world into which we have descended, the resurgence of White nationalism makes clear the underlying presumption of the Whiteness of America. The ghastly nature of this resurgence was most recently highlighted in the horrific White Supremacists' march in Charlottesville, VA, with tiki torches reminiscent of the KKK, and the mass shootings/terrorism at the Jewish Synagogue in Pittsburg, PA, which killed 26 and wounded many others. The idealization of our "White" nation allows little space for us to recognize, and thus make peace with, what an African American colleague of mine called the "painful underbelly of racism." *That which is not recognized and owned, cannot be mourned; reparations cannot be made, leaving us in a state of profound, perpetual melancholia, and a defensive grandiosity about our greatness/whiteness.* Additionally, the purified Whiteness of American Exceptionalism is achieved by projecting undesirable attributes into non-Whites, who are then trapped in a space where they are not considered "real Americans," often meaning less than human.

IV

About three years ago, the head of cultural programming at a Berlin museum, who had been touring the sights of our capital city, said to me, "It's so amazing to see how proud Americans are of their monuments. It's not like that for us in Germany." Somewhat mournfully she continued, "Our national monuments, great historic buildings ... they have all turned into symbols of shame for the horrible things we as a society have done." Her binary thinking, a good America and a bad Germany, struck a dissonant chord in me. I said, "Well, could not Americans also do with recognizing the mostly unacknowledged aspects of our own shameful past?"

The history of this country includes the genocide of Native American peoples and slavery of Black Americans. Our nation's greatness, enshrined in our national monuments, was made possible by the blood, sweat, and tears, as well as the ingenuity and creativity, of peoples who are barely a footnote in our history books and seldom represented in monuments depicting the greatness of America. Even today, Blacks, Hispanics, Native Americans, immigrants, women, sexual minorities, and members of other marginalized groups struggle for recognition; they struggle to be acknowledged, Jessica

Benjamin (1988) might say, as "equivalent subjects" of this great nation.

Recently, exposure of blatant and systematic violence and discrimination against Blacks and other racial minorities by the police and our justice system has pushed racism to the foreground. Donald Trump's presidential campaign used overtly racist tropes to garner votes during the 2016 election. It has moved us from dog whistles to bull horns! The meaning of a woman likely succeeding an African American president should be clear, as misogyny was also an ever-present aspect of Trump support. Obama's election had marked a transformational period for Americans, especially for African Americans and other peoples of color here and abroad. An African American couple, coming into our first session post-election, beamed and proclaimed, "We did it, Cherian! We did it!" I was touched and felt embraced by them in our otherness.

V

Unfortunately, in addition to more overt racism, we also see passive acceptance of racist attitudes by liberal Americans. Such attitudes are evidenced in subtler, at times even more destructive, forms of racism which include what John Dovidio calls "aversive racism," as well as the findings on implicit bias (go to: https://implicit.harvard.edu/implicit/ to take a sample test) and microaggressions (Sue, 2010). Dovidio (Dovidio and Gaertner, 2005) demonstrates, through his ingenious social psychology research, that since racism, sexism, and other isms are ego-alien to them, liberals are less likely to recognize their own biases, leading them to unconsciously act out biases for which they find justifications that cannot easily be unmasked. He found, for example, that when an African American collaborator in the study called for assistance, liberal-identified individuals hung up immediately upon hearing the African American-sounding voice, more frequently than did conservative-identified individuals. Such acts of discrimination among liberals have been found to be more common when their bias is not likely to be readily identified and when they can find other reasons for such discriminatory behaviors—"you are not a good fit," "best person for the job," etc. Such behaviors and attitudes were found even among those who spend considerable time in charity work for disadvantaged groups!

VI

Let me now turn to the in-between spaces occupied by Asian Americans in our melting pot of a culture. Asian Americans are considered a "model minority," a reference to the unusual level of academic and financial successes achieved by some, but hardly all, of the groups lumped into this category. For example, the success narratives regarding Indian, Korean, Chinese, and Japanese Americans neglect the crucial fact that members of those groups have been selectively allowed immigration (after an earlier period when this was not so), even recruited, for their already high academic and professional achievements. An even more sinister aspect of this idealizing (fetishizing?) of successful Asians is how they are then used to discredit claims of any real discrimination and racism in this country, especially against African Americans. An article in *New York Magazine* by Andrew Sullivan (2017) is an example par excellence of how this pernicious and discredited thinking is offered as proving the absence of racism in the United States. Sullivan states that, despite having experienced past racial discrimination, including lynching, the immigration exclusion act, and internment camps, "... today, Asian-Americans are among the most prosperous, well-educated, and successful ethnic groups in America. What gives? It couldn't possibly be that they maintained solid two-parent family structures, had social networks that looked after one another, placed enormous emphasis on education and hard work, and thereby turned false, negative stereotypes into true, positive ones, could it? It couldn't be that all whites are racists or that the American dream still lives?" (April 14, 2017). An outcome of thus becoming "honorary Whites" is that Asian Americans, as the Irish, the Italians, and the Jews before them, too often then discriminate, or are used to discriminate, against Blacks in identification with Whites, to hold onto their tenuous Whiteness!

VII

Immigrants and refugees continue to arrive in the United States, legally or not, with hopes that one day they and their offspring will become fully accepted as Americans, with equal opportunity to become who they can be—to live the promised American Dream. The narrative of the promised land held out the hope that with hard work and abiding by the laws of the land, anyone can succeed, attain citizenship, and their offspring may even become the president of the United States! Too often, such an ideal proves illusory, a fantasy of Whiteness, encountering constant "slippage" as the post-colonial critic Homi Bhabha (1994) suggests, almost there but never really white. Immigrants, especially those who are non-White, are repeatedly confronted with, "No, where are you *really* from?" That innocent-sounding question too often betrays the underlying presumption that as a non-White you cannot really be an American. The assumption is seen in the emboldened declarations of the White nationalists, "Jews will not replace us," and the taunting of persons of color to go back to where they come from, the Muslim ban and the separation of children from parents at the Mexican border. They show scant appreciation for the nature of this immigrant nation and the profound and beneficial aspects of diversity which make us unique in the world and perhaps should be what is truly exceptional about America.

As immigrants recognize the impossibility of achieving their American Dream—of Whiteness, perfection—they are confronted with a loss of this ideal. That loss is made more complicated by the continuing illusion of possibility, of "one day." Eng and Han (2000) call this process "racial melancholia," suggesting that it is unlike the Freudian notion of melancholia, which identifies a pathological intrapsychic process in conflicted grieving. Racial melancholia is marked by its cultural underpinnings, making it not entirely a pathological intrapsychic process, but instead also a cultural phenomenon with implications for intrapsychic and relational functioning. Eng and Han offer a heart-wrenching example of that phenomena in the life of a Japanese immigrant family. Soon after arriving in this country, their 5-year-old son found himself the object of scorn by classmates and teacher for the way he spoke certain English words—he had said them the way he had learned from his mother's Japanese-accented English. In time, the boy learned to speak more "proper" English as he struggled to be accepted in his new homeland by classroom peers and idealized teachers, while feeling shame for his mother's speech, the very same speech that had been soothing and affirming in the past. This child will have to come to grips with the cold reality that even as he grows up and succeeds in this country, working towards his American Dream, this highly Americanized Japanese American will learn that he is not to be seen as a "real" American! A Faustian bargain?

Aysha's Journey into Whiteness and Melancholia

Shortly after we began weekly psychotherapy sessions, Aysha, my 36-year-old Indian American patient, expressed her distress surrounding the blatantly discriminatory treatment African Americans received in the criminal justice system. On that particular day, an African American man was being prosecuted for drug related charges, and Aysha said, "I was looking around the courtroom, appalled to realize that everyone there was White, except for the defendant." Breathing in deeply, I said, "And then, there was you." She looked up at me, a bit startled. In that moment, I sensed that she may have felt recognized, interpellated, called out, into an otherness we shared, and she said, "Yes, then there is me. Isn't it interesting that I didn't see myself as also not White." Not White. And also, not Black, a point sharply brought to me by an African American colleague who said, "Cherian, we don't really consider you one of us. Actually, there is considerable resentment in our communities about the way Asian and other immigrants come to this country and get to move on ahead of us."

Until recently, Aysha told me, she had never thought of herself as having any issues around race or any other "serious" problems. She assured me that for most of her life she had been very happy, well adjusted. "But now, I am so unhappy, so ashamed of myself," Aysha said, weeping. "All this is because I cheated on my good husband. He is really a very good man." She explained that the week prior to the day she was to marry David, a White American, she began an affair with Derek, an African American co-worker, jeopardizing her marriage and her long-sought American dream. Six months into the marriage, her husband learned of the affair, precipitating a crisis.

Feeling passionately desired by Derek was affirming of her desirability as a woman, and for the first time in her life she enjoyed sex and even had her first orgasm. Additionally, she said, "I felt like I belonged in a way that I had never before felt. He wanted me all the time, like he worshipped my body!" Soon, it became clear that he was primarily interested in her as a sexual partner, perhaps even a fetishized object. "I know he is really a narcissist," she confessed. When he broke off the relationship, Aysha was devastated and quickly collapsed the space where pain could be experienced by becoming involved with yet another man, also Black. "Now I realize that I am only attracted to Black men. White guys are so boring, they don't do anything for me, sexually." As for South Asian men, Aysha was very clear: "Sex with Indian men, well, the very idea disgusts me." Her dark skinned, Indian American therapist wondered about the potential cultural, Oedipal, and transfererential meanings of this.

Aware of our community's colonial past which has left us with internalized racism with regards to our White colonizers, its denigrating attitudes towards Blacks in this country and our intra-cultural colorism, I wondered about their potential meaning for the very dark-skinned (Tummala-Narra, 2007) Aysha in relation to her father/family, as well as the meaning of her cuckolding her White husband. Working with someone from one's own cultural/racial/national origin is at once both familiar and challenging.

Race, Melancholia, and the Fantasy of Whiteness

Our internal family systems weave together the actual lived aspects of our immediate families and close kin within the larger context of our cultures and their deep-rooted histories. Whereas my Indian-ness allows for the possibility of recognizing aspects of my patient's cultural/historical situatedness, that familiarity can also create unwarranted collapsing of our experiential worlds, risking colluding to avoid our shared vulnerabilities, prejudices, and projections. Immigrant psychoanalyst Salman Akhtar's (2006) concept of "homo-ethnic transference" captures this dilemma, and it is especially true in cases where the numbers of one's reference group are relatively small.

Much later in our work, Aysha recalled vividly a scene from elementary school where her mother had made a point about their being Hindus and not Christian. She was raked with shame and wanted to hide. I commented, "You were painfully outed as outsider—not White, not Christian like the other children." This opened up more of the painful aspects of her growing up, experiences that had been walled off from conscious awareness. Her father's personal vulnerabilities appear to have been compounded by his lost ideal of the American dream. Having excelled in his career in North India, he had arrived in the United States with his young family with great hopes for himself and his children. As time went by, he became more and more desperate, not feeling seen, overlooked for promotions, and generally underappreciated as a promising scientist, perhaps experiencing a "brown-tinged glass ceiling." In a displacement of his narcissistic rage at unmet selfobject needs, father, who evidenced characterological challenges, became tyrannical at home where mother was not able to protect herself or her vulnerable children. Aysha found refuge in her school success, which provided her with some of the needed mirroring and idealizing selfobject experiences (Kohut, 1971), where cultural selfobjects were lacking. Her teachers delighted in such a bright, cooperative, and cheerful child, a child evidencing a tendency for "pathological accommodation" (Brandchaft, 2007).

"Once we got engaged," Aysha told me, "I knew that life would surely be perfect in the future as well." Married to a White man, she would finally have her American dream, a dream promised but perpetually denied her brown-skinned immigrant parents. Aysha told me she had imagined that any children she and David had together would be "Whiter" than she was, and by virtue of the greater Whiteness, more acceptable in society. In the generation after that, her grandchildren would be even more White and then, finally, "all my dark skin will be diluted away—they will just be white, Americans, acceptable." The clarity of her statement was startling, no place for me to hide from the melancholic acknowledgement of her perpetual otherness, an otherness she had earlier denied and dissociated from, in her idealized perfect childhood marked by the split-off nature of her cultural/racial identity. When I finally found my voice, recovering from my own reverie of struggles to feel acceptable, I told Aysha, "It's so sad hearing you, erasing yourself to be acceptable, even working toward making this dream become a reality for future generations." She just shrugged and said, "That's the reality, isn't it, Dr. Verghese?"

Aysha's heart-wrenching process of self-erasure and purification into Whiteness recalled to me Barbara Johnson's commentary on Anne Anlin Cheng's (2001) book *The Melancholia of Race*: "[This process] ...captures both the hidden melancholia of those who, in order to conform to the American dream, learn to discriminate against themselves and the *even more hidden melancholy of a nation thus deprived of some of the most vital energies of its citizens.*" Aysha had finally found herself at the threshold of fulfilling her American dream and progressively erasing her dark skin, the symbol of her otherness, through subsequent generations. Her bolting at the entrance to that mythical land of White perfection, causing a crisis in her marriage, acted out something she had never been able to express. It had not been consciously available for her to think about until she opened up in therapy. In fact, such internal conflicts had been masked by her performative perfections and a "not me" disavowal of her cultural/racial self. I viewed that move as a sign of a healthy ego refusing to suffocate the nascent sense of a true cultural, racial self, striving for recognition in its own right.   ▼

References

Akhtar, S. (2006). Technical challenges faced by the immigrant psychoanalyst. *Psychoanalytic Quarterly, 75*, 21-43.

Benjamin, J. (1988). *The bonds of love: Psychoanalysis, feminism, and the problem of domination*. New York: Pantheon Books.

Bhabha, H. (1994). *The location of culture*. New York: Routledge.

Bion, W. (1967). Notes on memory and desire. *The Psychoanalytic Forum, 2* (3).

Brandchaft, B. (2007). Systems of pathological accommodation and change in analysis. *Psychoanalytic Psychology, 24* (4): 667-687.

Cheng, A.A. (2001). *The melancholy of race: Psychoanalysis, assimilation, and hidden grief*. New York: Oxford University Press.

Cushman, P. (1995). *Constructing the self, constructing America: A cultural history of psychotherapy*. Boston: Da Capo Press.

DiAngelo, R. (2011). White fragility. *International Journal of Critical Pedagogy, 3* (3), 54-70.

Dovidio, J.F., & Gaertner, S. L. (2005). Color blind or just plain blind?: The pernicious nature of contemporary racism, *The Non Profit Quarterly. 12* (4).

Eng, D. & Han, S. (2000). A dialogue on racial melancholia. *Psychoanalytic Dialogues, 10* (4): 667.

Freire, P. (1968/1970). *Pedagogy of the oppressed*. Translated by Myra Bergman Ramos. New York: Bloomsbury.

Fanon, F. (1967/1994). *Black skin, white masks*. Translation by Constance Farrington. New York: Grove.

Gadamer, H. G. (1960). Truth and method. In Roger Frie and William Coburn (Eds. 1989). *Persons in context: The challenge of individuality in theory and practice*. New York: Routledge.

Gillman, S. (1993). *Freud, race, and gender*. Princeton, NJ: Princeton University Press.

Gump, J. (2010). Reality matters: the shadow of trauma on African American subjectivity. *Psychoanalytic Psychology, 27* (1): 42-54.

Holmes, D. (2006). The wrecking effects of race and social class on self and success. *Psychoanalytic Quarterly, 75* (1), 215-235.

Jones, A. & Oborne, M. (2014). Object fear: the national dissociation of race and racism in the era of Obama. *Psychoanalysis, Culture & Society, 19* (4), 392-412.

Kohut, H. (1971). *The analysis of the self*. International Universities Press.

Leary, K. (2006). In the eye of the storm. *Psychoanalytic Quarterly, 75*(1):345-363.

Lusane. C. (2010). *The black history of the White House*. San Francisco: City Lights.

Suchet, M. (2007). Unravelling whiteness. *Psychoanalytic Dialogues, 17* (6): 867-886.

Sue, D.W. (2010). *Microaggressions in everyday life: Race, gender, and sexual orientation*. Hoboken, NJ: Wiley.

Sullivan, A. (2017). Why do Democrats feel sorry for Hillary Clinton? *New York Magazine*, April, 14.

Tummala-Narra, P. (2007). Skin color and the therapeutic relationship. *Psychoanalytic Psychology, 24* (2):255-270.

Winograd, B. (2014). Black psychoanalysts speak. PEP Video Grants, 1 (1): 1.

I read Dr. Verghese's essay in the wake of the powerful 2018 AAP Institute and Conference titled *Sounds of Silence: Working the Edges of the Unspoken.* On the issue of race, the I&C focused on how to successfully navigate racial encounters, which otherwise often render even the most well-meaning people anxious and silent. Dr. Howard Stevenson's plenary on racial literacy emphasized and demonstrated how recognizing, tolerating, and using the anxiety generated by racial difference can facilitate successful and transformative contact between individuals across such a difference. Dr. Verghese's essay similarly makes an argument for the necessity to examine race and racial difference within our practice and field and thus dovetails nicely with the conversation started at the I&C.

Dr. Verghese's premise for his argument is the idea that our understanding of the world is heavily influenced by our collective historical narratives, and that these narratives differentially affect us based on our individual, cultural, historical, and national contexts. Within an increasingly multiracial and multicultural American society in general, and the field of psychotherapy in particular, meaningful contact across such differences would be possible if we could recognize our worldviews as prejudices that both limit and enable our ability to listen to other ways of looking at the world. Such contact, argues the author, drawing on Gadamer's *Truth and Method,* is potentially transformative, and hence essential, for all people involved. He supports his argument by first examining in different segments of his article the costs borne by the different oppressed groups within the various national and psychotherapy-specific narratives on race and racism, and then culminating in an evocative case example of racial melancholia (a term attributed by the author to David Eng and Shinhee Han) as a way to understand the experience of Asian Americans, whose personal and collective situatedness often engenders a worldview filled with a fantasy of Whiteness. This fantasy, with its often-illusory promise of success and recognition as "true" Americans, leads to an internalized denigration of their own cultural selves. Success then equates to disavowing the culturally-informed truths of their self and so creates an unfillable psychic void, an experience of racial melancholia. In his case example, Dr. Verghese and his Indian American patient, Aysha, within their co-created therapeutic space, slowly and courageously recognize her fantasy-filled worldview of Whiteness and the costs she bore as a result. From this process emerges the possibility for mourning and growth.

As I finished reading this essay, I was longing to know more about Dr. Verghese's own responses, how this experience of a "true conversation" with his patient transformed him. Perhaps, I imagine this essay is one of the outcomes of this contact. More importantly, my longing stems from a certain situatedness I share with the author; both of us are Western-educated immigrants from India. Aysha's experience in therapy filled me with sadness and hope as I could recognize my own mourning in her work. I was reminded of Salman Akhtar's (1994) seminal paper on the importance of mourning in acculturation, or what he calls the third individuation, of immigrants, whereby the splitting of the self and its relationship to the world, which results from the process of immigration, is mended through mourning that split and the losses inherent to immigration. From this process a transformed "new and hybrid identity" emerges (p. 1064).

While contemplating my response to Dr. Verghese's essay, the fact of our shared situatedness was present in more ways than were evident to me. Mostly focused on wanting to reflect the tradition of *Voices* and the Academy, I sought to write a personal reflective commentary on the article. I was *mostly* excited about that. However, while I was eager to respond to his article, I found myself paralyzed. Beating myself up from the approaching deadline, I felt conflicted over what should I write about, how should I write about it, and so on. Two aspects emerged as I grappled with this conflict. It became clear to me that part of my excitement was about responding to Dr. Verghese, or *Cherian.* Although I am deeply connected to the Academy personally and professionally, seeing an article from another Indian immigrant made me aware of how I have been longing for a "homoethnic" connection (Akhtar, 2009) within the Academy. Sharing my honest reactions and responses to his essay with him offered the possibility of, even if only vicariously and imperfectly, fulfilling this desire.

Although the recognition of my longing freed up some of the ideas I have shared above, I was left with a very uncomfortable and uncanny feeling, *the feeling of being watched*. Of being watched by a White audience that would compare, judge, reward, or dismiss. Suddenly, Cherian and I became less of the desired kinsmen bonding and uniting over our mutual exchange of feelings, agreements, and disagreements about his essay, but more as gladiators trying to vie for the crown of "model minority" citizens, combating in the arena of *Voices*, where our ideas transformed into swords would help us slice our way to survival and victory, while entertaining the larger non-immigrant AAP readership. His article and my commentary were transformed into matters of pride and shame. I fantasized about giving up on writing a response. But, alongside the violence and tragedy of my imagination, there was an unignorable sensuousness and passion of the imagery of gladiators. As if suddenly, I look up in the stadium and I see the actual faces of people whom I know, respect, and love, rather than my fantasized audience. A new reality sets in as the sensuousness pulls centerstage the retreating excitement of connecting with Cherian; a new truth emerges.

I feel grateful to both Cherian and to *Voices* for this experience. This thought-provoking article, even if I wasn't able to fully understand its use of segmentation, also helped me appreciate the 2018 I&C in a new light: as an example of the Academy's effort to have difficult—but vitally important to our mission of seeking our truths as psychotherapists and as an organization—"true conversations" about several shame-laden and contextually problematic issues that define us as individuals and as members of one or many groups. What other truths does the analogy of gladiators symbolize about this process of "conscientization," which Dr. Verghese, *Voices*, and the Academy have undertaken?

— Samir M. Patel, MD MPH

References:

Akhtar, S. (2009). Friendship, socialization, and the immigrant experience. *Psychoanalysis, Culture & Society, 14,* 253–272.

Akhtar, S. (1994). A third individuation: Immigration, identity, and the psychoanalytic process. *Journal of the American Psychoanalytic Association, 43,* 1051-84.

Stevenson, H. (2018, October). If elephants could talk: Racial literacy to manage stress in face-to-face encounters. Plenary presented at the Institute and Conference of the American Academy of Psychotherapists, Atlanta, GA.

▼

A Therapist Meets a Former Patient

James Carpenter

The secrets of others live young and fresh,
Spring forth after twenty criss-crossed years.
I meet her pounding away on the elliptical
In my gym. Back in town for Christmas.
Sudden smiles, adult handshake,
Her words tumble, "I remember
Going out to your office" and "I survived my adolescence."
Behind the steel machines there is all
She doesn't say and I don't say but both of us remember clearly,
These things peep out
And wish to not be called. As I protect
The confidentiality of anyone I protect
Her from herself and she colludes with my collusion.
Millions of separate moments gone as burned
up leaves, but the secrets bright and green.

Pictures of her children
On her phone, the tolerable
Routine commuting on the Metro,
"I turned out fairly normal."
She feels an impulse to fill me in on the unsaid-
to-anyone, the affair perhaps
Or her mother's suicide attempt
Or the wish to run farther away than this
From home – or none of this.
Whatever it might be it turns back from the brink
Of saying, more smiles
Goodbye Goodbye.
Secrets tender as the smiles
Of children take up a place
In the elliptic of a poem.

Bonnie Buchele

Trauma of These Times:
A Presenter's Personal Struggle

I REALLY WANTED TO DO THIS, BUT I WAS HAVING TROUBLE. Emotional life in groups had been fascinating, stimulating, and satisfying all of my professional life. As social and political chaos in the United States grew, beginning with the 2016 presidential campaign, I watched, noting to myself that what was going on was large group dynamics of the first order; then I would quickly turn to other matters, usually with relief. When I was invited to be the keynote speaker at a conference about this stressful, even traumatic, environment and its impact on therapists and groups, I found myself surprised, intrigued, and intimidated. I was surprised because I live in the Midwest far from Washington, DC. I knew my background studying trauma was a primary reason for the invitation, but I also was intimidated since I do not live "inside the Beltway" and could be seen as not being fully informed.

I felt honored to be invited and so, despite my misgivings, narcissism prevailed, and I accepted. Hovering in the background was a less conscious motivation: I had not realized how troubled I was by the turmoil showing up in my office and creeping into my mind. I hoped to find ways to help my patients and to settle myself. So, over a year before the conference, I set about writing the four plenaries I had agreed to present.

Much to my surprise, I found it difficult to sit down and begin the process. I found other things to do, and the time set aside to write would be gone. Finally, I forced myself to sit at the computer, only to go blank. I could not decide how to begin or what to say. I have grown comfortable, even found pleasure over the years, making presentations about my work; I have some confidence and

BONNIE J. BUCHELE, PhD, ABBP, DFAGPA, is a psychologist, group psychotherapist, and psychoanalyst in Kansas City, Missouri. She serves on the executive council of the American Psychoanalytic Association, is a past president and distinguished fellow of the American Group Psychotherapy Association, and is past director and current faculty member of the Greater Kansas City Psychoanalytic Institute. Following 30 years at the Menninger Clinic, she served as consultant to clinicians working with survivors of 9/11. Dr. Buchele has published on subjects ranging from trauma to group psychotherapy to psychoanalysis, while lecturing, teaching, and consulting within the USA and internationally.
bonniebuchele@gmail.com

experience doing that. But this was different. It was about my work in the larger world and I could not find the old, familiar excitement.

Though I try to keep up with the news, I am not a news junkie; I do not even consider myself well-informed. I watch the news as I exercise every morning, and I read the Kansas City Star every night, so I know what is happening in the world, but I am not an expert. I thought I would begin by making a list of events during the campaign and since the election that had been distressing to me, the people in my world, and to some extent perhaps, the world in general. But it was well into 2017 by this time and a lot had happened. The list was much longer than I remembered. I tried to put what had happened into words, but I could not find the right words. As I reflected, I discovered that the "right" words were ways of describing what had happened without offending anyone. It seemed impossible to do. I turned to outside sources to stimulate my memories and thoughts, but newspapers and sources online all seemed to be written with a bias one way or another, and often the bias was not acknowledged by the source. By now I thought I could not trust the veracity of anything I was reading; wariness was required. This went on for weeks.

Trying to help myself out of this paralyzed and helpless state, I asked my husband (a lawyer) to sit down with me and make the list. I even had trouble taking that step, because I feared that he and I would disagree about how to describe the events and trends that were contributing factors. But at last I began and felt a little relief. As we talked about it together, I realized how much I had repressed, how it was difficult to remember details. He remembered helpful details, but when I would get back to it on my own, repression would set in again. I was full of feeling, fearful of describing things in a biased or ignorant way. I had trouble thinking and for a while could only write and speak in unsophisticated language—without nuance or detail, fearful that I would unknowingly commit a microaggression, which would leave me feeling embarrassed and humiliated.

I continued to work on that list, repeatedly experiencing episodes of anxiety as I forced myself to double down with the deadline approaching. I decided to take a break from the initial presentation with its elusive, dreaded list. I realized that if I titrated my exposure to the subject matter, I might be able to think more clearly. I was rewarded: for the first time there was a crack in my paralyzed state, and I felt ok giving myself a respite. Still, I could not come up with a cogent explanation as to why this task was so arduous and unremittingly demanding.

In a rare and fleeting moment of reflection, I had the thought that surveying my local colleagues might help to free me up and move me along. I constructed that brief survey and sent it out. I was pleased when many answered, responding about how much they were hearing—multiple times daily—about the turmoil in the world. I was curious that I had started to feel a little bit better. I had not realized how isolated and alone I felt, trying to think about these things and manage my own anxiety, rage, confusion, and sense of helplessness. More often than I cared to know, I had lost my capacity to think.

I began to think again. With that development came a wish to understand what was happening from a theoretical point of view. So I read Bion, Nitsun, Kernberg, Post, Gilligan, Kimmel, Schore, Dluhy, Segalla and others. Bright lights would come on when a theory helped to explain some aspect of what the world and I were experiencing. It became clear that polarization within the society was rampant. We have two choices when a discussion becomes polarized: shut down, fearful of being attacked for our point of view, or blame the other person out of frustration. Both choices lead to further polarization as well as to increased rage and helplessness. There is a way out of those two alternatives, I learned as I studied: When one tries to put oneself in the experience of the other, to be empathic, the conversation has some chance of going in a better direction. I tried this intervention in my personal and professional life, and it helped me to understand the position of the other person. Then I could listen. I could think again, and gradually I felt calmer.

Still, new feelings of despair would set in because events kept happening—the Kavanaugh hearings, the mail bombs, the shootings and killings at the Tree of Life Synagogue. Would it never stop? Those feelings of despair and polarization seemed to be everywhere; sometimes it was difficult even to manage living in the mildly polarized positions within my own family. I had anxious episodes again as I doubled down on the work with the deadline looming.

I decided I would return to that first plenary with its dreaded list and try to put the factors contributing to the turbulence into some sort of order. But I was unable to find any order. These factors just seemed to be a hodge-podge of events, trends, reactions. Finally, I realized that I was feeling overwhelmed as I tried to describe the traumatizing conditions; my attempt to order them was a stab at gaining mastery. On a smaller scale, I was reliving what was happening in the United States as I tried to write. I thought, maybe it would be helpful for plenary participants to taste a little of my experience. Maybe I should let go of trying to order the chaos, give participants a soft warning, and let the thoughts and descriptions of all the contributing factors flow. Perhaps in an experiential way they, too, could feel the confusion and painful paralysis but then gain some understanding of what is happening to all of us.

I also realized that my inability to find the right words had to do with my attempt to preempt hurting someone on one side or another as I tried to open a psychological space for us to think about this together. I might use the wrong words, they would be offended or feel left out, and I would feel incompetent and guilty for having caused pain. I might become the object of a powerful negative transference from which I feared I might be unable to extricate myself constructively. Finally, I thought that, in fact, this perception of me as biased, incompetent, provocative, or polarizing was likely to happen, and we would just need to process it and try to work it through. I also realized that I do have a point of view and it will unavoidably show from time to time. I cannot sterilize my mind or become a robot. What I can do is be open to hearing differing experiences and opinions. I can try to empathize without losing myself. If we all did that, maybe the polarization would decrease.

These are difficult times. Whenever traumatic events happen, the effects do not only lead to pain and suffering, which must be our focus at the beginning. Traumatic experiences also often bring the opportunity for new growth because the rules are all turned on their heads. I have experienced and seen this over and over. But I had had to go through a disorienting, overwhelming experience as I tried to make sense of it. At last I remembered that trauma also brings the opportunity for creative change. Temporarily I had lost the space in my mind to hold this awareness, but now the capacity to think and have hope was back. ▼

Rhona Engels

The Abiding American Character:
2018, Twelve Years Later

EARLIER THIS YEAR MY WALLET WAS STOLEN AND I LOST MY GREEN CARD IDENTIFYING ME AS A PERMANENT ALIEN IN THE UNITED STATES. I applied for a new one but was told that I could travel internationally only if I presented myself in person at the immigration office to have my Canadian passport stamped. Scheduling an appointment had to be done online. I quickly discovered that there were a vast number of desperate people trying to do the same thing only to reach the inevitable message, "No appointments available." Later I would discover that this is because the Trump administration has shifted resources to enforcement, starving areas designed to help people. Having the resources of a middle class person, I was able to hire a young, competent, and impassioned immigration lawyer. She accompanied me to the immigration office, negotiated the sometimes indifferent, sometimes hostile layers of bureaucracy, and within an hour I had the precious stamp, a small smudge in my passport marking the difference between helpless entrapment and freedom.

As if that weren't enough to underline my newly discovered vulnerability, she warned me that under the present administration, should I get arrested for any reason and be unable to produce physical evidence of my status, I could have my green card revoked and find myself in some danger of deportation. So much for 51 years of living and paying taxes in this country. She advised naturalization, so I did some research and discovered that it would require an in-depth investigation of my taxes, work, and personal life. I told her I had some concern about making myself so visible. To my surprise, she agreed. She thought the risk was small, but in the atmosphere of the present

RHONA ENGELS, LCSW, ACSW, has been in private practice for 34 years working with individuals, couples and groups, and providing supervision. She is retired as associate professor in the Graduate School of Social Work of New York University and as faculty of several psychoanalytic institutes. She has published articles in *Voices* and other clinical journals, served on the Executive Council of AAP for 13 years, and holds dearly the honor of Fellow of the organization. *rhonae1@gmail.com* administration, not negligible. Worst case scenario, if something were found that Immigration Services didn't like, I could have my green card revoked and be threatened with deportation. I could at least appreciate the irony that the term "catch-22" had originated in America. I decided I was better off lying low and making sure I keep my green card very safe.

What I discovered in losing my green card is an unexpected vulnerability, not just as an expat, but as a member of the 99%. Unless you are part of the 1%, you are vulnerable, not just financially, but in other ways that none of us would care to admit. This realization prompted me to re-read "The Abiding American Character," an article I wrote and had published in a 2006 issue of *Voices*. This was two years before the housing mortgage, banking, and market crash and well before Trump was anywhere on the scene. Re-reading it 12 years later and as someone who had never before written a psychological/political piece, I found myself astonished, depressingly so, at how abiding it is. I had described competing tensions in the American psyche between concern for the collective on the one hand, and an every-man-for-himself attitude on the other, suggesting that the latter was intensifying. Twelve years later, it seems to me that this process has continued and greatly accelerated.

This swing of the pendulum leaves many facing relentless struggles, if not dire circumstances. As therapists, it is part of our job to face and to help our patients face hard realities. "Psychoanalysis," Adam Phillips (1997) writes, "is a theory of the unbearable, of what one prefers not to know" (p.13). In present day America, what we prefer not to know may be less about individual pathology and more about facing the end of upward mobility, the corruption, indifference, and incompetence of government, the fragmentation of information, and the ever increasing dominance of every-man-for-himself, which produces a societal atmosphere that becomes immune to compassion or effective concern for the other.

A patient who recently lost her mother came in furious with her insurance company. She pays a high premium for a policy that offers out-of-network benefits. The company had decided to reimburse her for my services at the cheaper Medicare rate even though, at 57, she isn't even eligible for the program. This is illegal, but in the present political climate there is little oversight, and she is unlikely to get anywhere without enormous expense of time and money.

Back in the day, certainly before I lost my green card, I might have considered her rage a defense against the helpless grief of her huge loss, which of course it partly is. But, I said nothing other than some version of "that sucks." Once her rage died down, she said, "Underneath all this, I'm heartbroken. I can't find my mother anywhere. She was the only one I felt tethered to, and without her I don't know what to do with myself or how to live. And that so many people in charge are shitty makes it so much worse." Precisely. I think we therapists need to attend to both the internal and external realities, knowing that the present day realities in this country make it so much worse for so many.

That the generosity of the American spirit, a concern for the welfare of all, has receded seems painfully obvious and much truer now than when I wrote about it 12 years ago. Yet, I must include at least some encouraging signs. There are the recent courageous efforts by younger people, mostly women and minorities, running for office and trying to shift the political system back in the direction of concern for the collective. There is a rising awareness of the myth of self determinism. Zach Wood (2018), a young African

American writer, recently wrote, "My experience has taught me that pulling yourself up by your bootstraps is a myth. Achieving social mobility requires far more than will and ability. It's nearly impossible to rise without other people helping you pull yourself up."

Perhaps the most important thing I have learned from my green card experience and re-reading "The Abiding American Character" is to stay alert to the unbearable, to all the implications of every-man-for-himself on us, our families, our friends, and our patients. Let us acknowledge that the systemic adversities are real weights on our lives and not just defenses against dealing with characterological conflicts. Let us acknowledge that the pursuit of happiness and pulling yourself up by your bootstraps, already harsh ideals, have, in the world of every-man-for-himself, receded like Gatsby's vision, and that the cards are increasingly stacked. Let us validate our patients' legitimate anger at these multiple systemic failures, rather than inadvertently intensify their self-blame with its resulting despair, bitterness, displaced revenge, and resignation. Legitimate and validated anger can carry hope and energy to fight for change. ▼

References:

Phillips, A. (1997). *Terrors and experts*. Cambridge: Harvard University Press.

Wood, Z. (2018, August 28). Lessons from 2000 hours on a public bus. *The New York Times*. Retrieved online at https://www.nytimes.com/2018/08/28/opinion/lessons-from-2000-hours-on-a-public-bus.html

The Abiding American Character   *Winter, 2006*

SEVERAL WEEKS AGO, WHILE LISTENING TO AN INTERVIEW WITH AN EXPERT ON COMICS, I LEARNED THAT COMIC BOOK SUPERHEROES ARE AN AMERICAN INVENTION AND AN ALMOST EXCLU-SIVELY AMERICAN PASSION. This sparked my desire to explore the "abiding self" of national, rather than individual character, specifically the American belief in individual freedom and empowerment and its implications for us, our patients, our profession and our overall sense of well-being.

I would like to make it clear at the outset that the goal of this article is not to change anyone's value system. As happens in bad psychotherapy, any effort to transform deeply held principles or ideals leads inevitably to a power struggle. I offer speculation and opinions, but no Answers. If anything, I think we suffer from an overabundance of Answers, which however well meaning, promote the very polarization they are meant to resolve. Instead, I would like to consider what the present static—red versus blue, conservative versus liberal, my "facts" versus your "facts"—is "designed to exclude," as Adam Phillips puts it (*Terrors and Experts*, p. 32). What might such intense polarization serve to distract us from? My goal here is to promote empathic curiosity. We are embedded in shared history and an even deeper, more complex value system or "abiding self" that envelops us all.

Contemplating this topic, I puzzled over a socio-political contradiction: an ever accelerating income gap in America so that middle and upper-middle class households have seen their real income rise very little since the late 1970s compared with the income of the richest 1% which has roughly doubled. In my opinion, the policies of the current administration have tended to favor the interests of this tiny, wealthy minority over everyone else. Why, I wondered, hasn't at least a sizable minority of that 99% protested, taken to the streets, rushed to the polls, flooded the media? It occurred to me that if you believe, like Horatio Alger, that you are free to do and achieve whatever you want, that almost everything depends on individual capacity and will, then if you are part of that 1% it means you have the smarts, the will, etc., and you've earned it. On the other hand, if you are part of the other 99% especially the lower part, then it's because you lack the will, smarts, and other capacities necessary for success, and it's your fault. Under this belief system, even if you consciously blame your government, parents, or God, you are likely to blame yourself as well, consciously or unconsciously, with the usual resulting shame and self-hatred. Either way, you are unlikely to complain.

In addition, there's the weight of self-fulfilling prophecy whereby you unwittingly perpetuate the "reality" that corresponds to the belief system without realizing its source in the national psyche. Your internal judge then has proof either of your worthiness or your unworthiness, you're a winner or a loser; if the former, you've earned it, if the latter, it's your own damned fault. If you find yourself in the latter category, how would you access the confidence to confront social-political injustice based on a national belief system of which you are a part? It is far more likely that you will live secretly ashamed and either alienated from the political process, or supporting the very ideal that helps crush you. This ideal seems to promise success, if only you will "pull yourself up," perhaps get therapy, so that you can do and become whatever you want. The pervasiveness and comprehensiveness of this belief system are such that you are likely to subscribe to it no matter where you locate yourself on the socio-political spectrum.

After my divorce when I was 38 and my daughter was 6, my parents expressed dismay that I might never have a fur coat. It was assumed that as a divorced, struggling, middle-class woman, I would unlikely afford one for myself, but even if I could (there was never any question that I would want it), not having a fur coat was a shameful admission of failure. A fur coat, like steak, a new Cadillac every two years, and marriage to a professional, was a shining symbol of middle-class success. The weight of the symbolic coat hung far heavier on me than any fur coat I could have owned. In addition to the grief I felt at the dissolution of my marriage, for many years I carried the weight of believing I had failed as wife, mother, daughter and professional. I even allowed my parents to buy me a fur coat. It's unsurprising that I had little motivation to fight or even to notice the weight of the belief system that contributed to my shame and feelings of inadequacy. In accordance with the law of self-fulfilling prophecy, participating in this belief system actually interfered with my achieving the success that could have disproved it.

The trouble is that the American ideal of individual empowerment and freedom also provides a compelling, positive and powerful inspiration. American "can do" has no doubt contributed to this country's enormous productivity. As a beacon of hopes and dreams, strength and invulnerability, it has drawn generations of immigrants ground down by the weight of history's dark side. Soon after 9/11, I spoke with my Israeli cousin who lives in Jerusalem. He said that he and many Israelis were grieving not only for those who had lost their lives and for their loved ones, but for their own lost hope. "In all we have been through in this country" he said, "we always keep in mind that America is invulnerable and free from all this. Now, if we can't bear what goes on here, where can we go?"

It occurs to me as I write this, that my cousin, like so many outside the US, may have bought, indeed may need to buy America's idealistic vision of itself as special and unique, "A City on a Hill" as former President Reagan put it. Inhabitants of those countries that emphasize collective responsibility may feel stifled and long for the American ideal of individual freedom and opportunity without being aware of a certain obliviousness and insensitivity toward them contained in this point of view. That the US has thought of itself as elevated is strikingly evident in the response to the 9/11 attacks. Repeated reference is made to "the post 9/11 world," the "new age of terrorism," but what gets ignored is that most of the rest of the world has been experiencing even deadlier forms of terrorism for a long time.

> Nancy, a charming, highly articulate young woman came to see me recently, complaining of loneliness, emptiness, lethargy and self-loathing, though she functions reasonably well at her job and reports that she has many friends. Soon after we started working together she was laid off, decided to "start over," and suddenly moved away to be closer to her family. She said that she wanted to better connect with them partially as a result of what she was learning and feeling in therapy. Unfortunately, it was too early in the therapy to effectively explore all the dynamics involved and I agreed to phone sessions at least until she got settled. Soon after, I discovered that she hadn't paid the psychiatrist to whom I had referred her. I told her that our "contract" was very important to me and that I could not continue to work with her if I couldn't trust her to uphold it. She responded immediately, paid my bill on time and called the psychiatrist to apologize and promised payment. Several weeks later, she has not paid the psychiatrist, missed her phone session with me, and it is uncertain whether I will hear further from her or receive this month's payment.

It would be too easy, I think, to write her off as "sociopathic." I believe her response to me was genuine, if ambivalent. She seemed touched that I would care enough to expect her to live up to her commitment to me and to the psychiatrist. However, underlying her depression and self-loathing there is, I believe, a sense of specialness, an angry entitlement which has as its source emotional deprivation, lack of or bad attachment. In turn this fuels revenge for having received bad parenting, some version of "you owe me." I propose that the US's idealized self-image as special and unique, which can truly dazzle, inspire and empower, also includes, like my patient, a lack of curiosity about and empathy for others that may, like her, have as their source a tenuous connection and attachment.

Another element of the dark side of the American belief in individual empowerment includes an "every man for himself" attitude that teaches a lack of empathy and a disinclination to assume any responsibility for the well being of others, another aspect of what might be labeled "national narcissism." Collective responsibility gets short shrift. National narcissism leads to the assumption that government has no obligation to be at least partially responsible for our quality of life. This might explain why the US is the only "first world" country without national health insurance. The assumption seems to be that this is an individual rather than collective responsibility, a privilege rather than a right, and that social programs inevitably encourage dependence and entitlement and destroy individual incentive.

"Every man for himself" also produces an extreme form of competition based on envy and threat of failure. Since we experience everything through the lens of this belief system, we assume that this form of competition is ubiquitous, rather than engendered by the belief system itself. There is no doubt a universal urge to compete and to compare ourselves with others. Generally, comparing favorably makes us happy, while comparing poorly generates envy, a sense of shame and inadequacy. In countries where the majority of people are very poor but less than they used to be, people report feeling optimistic and happy as they anticipate an even better future and more important, are surrounded by people of similar position, thus minimizing envy. It's not surprising that reports of increasing unhappiness in the US parallel rising inequality and decreasing upward mobility. Perhaps this situation fuels an anxious drive to prevent failure as defined by the ideal. I believe that such a frantic pursuit of individual freedom eventually constrains upward mobility and thus curtails and disappoints the very promise it holds out.

This extreme form of competition, along with actual decreased upward mobility gets further intensified, in my opinion, by the fact that risk and entrepreneurship, parts of the ideal of individual empowerment, have become a more essential part of the American psyche than ever before. Many Americans have experienced diminished job security, health benefits, and pension plans, while the old mechanisms of mitigating risk—trade unions and paternalistic corporations—are in decline. Author Thomas Edsall (*Building Red America: The New Conservative Coalition and the Drive for Permanent Power*) asserts that "the pervasiveness of risk in today's economy has made many Americans feel it is safer to look out for yourself and your kin than to place your fate in the hands of a politically controlled collective" (p. 52).

Individual striving, the glorification of independence, and "every man for himself" minimize or dismiss the importance of attachment and community. In a recent column, "Of Human Bonding," neo-con David Brooks, decries the lack of emphasis in the US on human attachment. He writes that "attachment theory has been thriving for decades, but it's had little impact on public policy." He concludes that "maybe it's time to focus a little less on individual capacities and more on nurturing attachment" (2006).

The American ideal of individual empowerment and freedom thus has the capacity to inspire and to cut down, to lift up and to shame, to seduce and to disappoint. At the end of F. Scott Fitzgerald's *The Great Gatsby*, the quintessential novel about the American dream, Nick, the narrator, sits brooding on the beach of the "huge incoherent failure" of Gatsby's estate: "I thought of Gatsby's wonder when he first picked out the green light of Daisy's dock. …Gatsby believed in the green light, the orgiastic future that year by year recedes before us. It eluded us then but no matter—tomorrow we will run faster, stretch out our arms farther" (p. 182).

I believe that this core aspect of the American psyche affects powerfully—for better and for worse—our work as psychotherapists. In general, we have become more aware of and sensitive to the impact of culture, gender, etc., on us and our patients. However, I think we tend to be less aware of the influence of the American ideal of individual empowerment, freedom and responsibility. On the one hand, without this belief our profession would have no reason to exist. How could we be effective? How could we offer realistic hope that our patients have some say over their lives and therefore that their efforts at self exploration and change are worthwhile? Perhaps it is because of the optimism and hope generated by such a strong belief in individual empowerment that the psychotherapy profession has thrived more in America than anywhere else. I can think of no other country with such a proliferation of self-help theories and problem-solving orientations.

On the other hand, as in the greater society, I think this belief system has become too extreme. For example, some psychotherapists believe that an inability to pay their fee is inevitably a matter of choice or part of individual pathology. They may make it a matter of principle never to adjust their fee so as not to "enable" their patients' self-victimization or entitlement. I think there is some rationalizing in this explanation and a defensive component in refusing a case-by-case determination. Perhaps shifting the responsibility so exclusively to the patient conceals some guilt about admitting the gratification, financial and otherwise in holding so firmly to the fee. The effect may be antithetical to the therapeutic goal of empowering the patient, exacerbating the very pathology being treated. The salt of the overwhelming sense of individual failure and shame gets rubbed into the character wound inflicted by the belief system under which the therapist operates.

After my patient, Fran, readily agreed to my fee, it took several months for me to become aware that she was struggling financially. She is in her mid-twenties, in her first job after college. When I asked her why it hadn't occurred to her to inquire whether I would consider temporarily lowering my fee, she told me that she had actually preferred to struggle, anything rather than become "troublesome" to me, like her sister, and therefore no longer the "good" girl she felt she needed to be to get what little nurturing she could from her parents. Had my fee been nonnegotiable, I might have unwittingly helped to replicate the very childhood experience that brought her into treatment.

Shelly Kopp's "Eschatological Laundry List" is a striking example of the fine line between empowering and shaming. Even though he states that "we must live within the ambiguity of partial freedom" (37) and forgive ourselves "again and again," (43) he also writes that "We are responsible for everything that we do." (34) "No excuses will be accepted," (35) as if there could be no legitimate reasons other than individual responsibility. It seems to me that his point of view is colored by that too extreme American ideal, and doesn't seriously enough consider the complexity of "partial freedom."

Maria, a patient of mine, possesses an amazing life force in the face of a calamitous childhood we don't often encounter in the "first world." She was born in a South American jungle and saw her first white man at the age of five when American missionaries arrived. Before she was 18, her father abandoned the family and was imprisoned for killing a woman with a machete, a sister died of malnutrition, she learned to kill rats for food, worked as an indentured servant for a family that abused her, and had been raped. Somehow, she persevered. In her early 20s she wrote then President Carter explaining her dream to come to America. He was so taken with her eloquence that he sponsored her emigration to the US (I have read the letters). Working in New York as a seamstress and a housekeeper, she participated in an "Est" seminar where it was hammered home to her that she was responsible for everything in her life. I met her shortly thereafter on the psychiatric inpatient unit to which she had been admitted with a brief acute psychotic episode induced by her "Est" weekend. Her sense of overwhelming responsibility had literally driven her crazy.

Perhaps we can more fully grasp the power of the "Horatio Alger" ideal if we examine more closely what this myth "is designed to exclude" (Phillips, 1997). Consider another aspect of the ideal, American resilience, the ability to dust oneself off and keep going. Admirable and productive though it is, I think it comes at the price of forgetfulness. I recall the outpouring of need to connect, to lend solace or a hand immediately after 9/11 and how quickly and profoundly it spread throughout the country and the world. Too soon after 9/11 though, when President Bush was asked "how much of a sacrifice Americans should be expected to make in their daily lives," he answered "Our hope is that they make no sacrifice whatsoever."

National narcissism wasn't always so extreme. Traditionally in this country, the ideal of freedom and independence has coexisted with a profound compassion for others. Every immigrant coming by ship to America passed by the words "Give me your tired, your poor, your huddled masses longing to breathe free." During the Depression, FDR said, "We now realize as we never have realized before our interdependence on each other; that we cannot merely take but we must give as well; that if we are to go forward, we must move as a well trained and loyal army willing to sacrifice for the good of a common discipline because without such discipline no progress is made, no leadership becomes effective." And similarly, Lincoln at the end of the civil war said "with charity for all and malice toward none."

However, it is important to keep in mind that the underlying fluctuations in the American psyche, between individual empowerment and freedom on the one hand and collective concern on the other, transcend politics. Underlying our stark and polarized political differences, I believe there exist "equal opportunity" tensions in the American psyche that cross and envelop all political persuasions. Compassion for others and policies based on it may have been more evident during the Lincoln and FDR administrations. Nonetheless, Lincoln too, suspended habeas corpus and the FDR administration was responsible for the infamous policy of internment of thousands of Japanese citizens, not so different from the present administration's proposed policies on habeas corpus and the treatment of "unlawful combatants." Just like the tension in the American psyche between the longing for freedom without ties and the longing for roots and attachment, I think another source of these policies lies in a similar tension between an exuberant, trusting optimism and confidence on the one hand, and enormous fear, suspicion and vulnerability on the other, another tension present from the beginning of this nation.

It may seem, post 9/11, that US fears of terrorism are well founded and that all the attempts to address it are realistic. However, I would suggest that the response goes well beyond the realistic threat and points to an underlying tendency to fear, vulnerability and mistrust. The US is preparing to build a fence on the US-Mexico border to prevent illegal immigration and possible terrorist infiltration. It is almost as if the American psyche has needed an external enemy to rationalize its sense of fear and vulnerability. How else to explain the excesses of the McCarthy era, the frantic search for the communists in our midst and elsewhere?

Just as a trusting optimism has coexisted with an underlying fear and suspicion, the pursuit of individual empowerment, freedom and responsibility has traditionally operated alongside an essential, if secondary ideal of compassion and collective responsibility.

I am reminded of the movie, *Shane*, the story of a cowboy, a loner with a longing for attachment, a rescuer and a hero like Superman, tempted by romantic love, family and community, who ultimately chooses the romance of freedom and isolation. Road movies, too, are essentially American. This restless mobility and romance with the open road have engendered enormous creativity and productivity, but, I believe, at the expense of fragmenting families and eroding a sense of community.

In my practice, I have met many, men especially, who vacillate between a longing for marriage and family, and the romantic appeal of freedom from all ties, or what popularly gets labeled as "fear of commitment." It seems to be taken for granted, at least by the American middle class, that their children leave home to attend college elsewhere and then often settle in some other part of the country, an unusual state of affairs elsewhere in the world. This scattering further erodes the foundation of connectedness on which a sense of collective empathy or caring is built.

Communities are continually dissolved and newly reformed, and as such are fragile and susceptible to erosion. In more recent times, I believe that the demise of the draft contributed enormously to this erosion. In gathering men from all socioeconomic and geographical backgrounds, the draft created a community that had a profound integrating effect on American society while emphasizing the necessity for shared sacrifice. The egalitarian ideal of shared sacrifice was then further eroded during the Johnson administration through policy changes that tried to persuade people that sacrifice was unnecessary, that they could have both "guns and butter." More recently still, though the country is on a war footing, there has been no revival of the draft with the result that the war effort is supported disproportionately by ethnic groups, rural people and the poor. Economically, instead of shared sacrifice, there have been massive tax cuts whose benefits have gone overwhelmingly to the very rich.

Also, it seems axiomatic that freedom of the individual and equality, or concern for the collective, cannot be equally pursued. Sweden, for example, emphasizes concern for the collective and therefore puts considerable constraints on individual liberty in the form of high taxes. This enforces greater equality at the expense of individual opportunity and freedom, and in return provides collective stability and safety. Nonetheless, I believe that while the US has traditionally emphasized individual freedom, the most extreme implications of this value system have traditionally been kept in check, however tenuously, by, among other things, an active concern for those outside one's family and group, and for the common good.

However, accelerated by post 9/11 fears, it seems to me that the American ideals of individual freedom and power, along with underlying fear, mistrust and vulnerability have, once again, grown at the expense of collective empathy. Just how far the national psyche has deviated yet again from its traditional compassion, is reflected in the policy of "extraordinary rendition" and a push, once again, to suspend habeas corpus for some non-citizens held in US custody outside the United States. This right, to demand that even the highest officials in a nation justify the detention of a human being, is one that would seem to be an essential part of America's identity as a free society, and a crucial check on injustice. Speaking at a congressional hearing, Gen. James Walker, the top uniform lawyer for the Marines, said that no civilized country denies defendants the right to see the evidence against them. The United States, he said, "should not be the first." Senator Lindsay Graham, a conservative South Carolina Republican and former military judge said, "it would be unacceptable, legally, in my opinion, to give someone the death penalty in a trial where they never heard the evidence against them." (*NY Times,* 9/10/06). Considering that there is also a push toward allowing some forms of interrogation that satisfy most definitions of torture, is there not some strange sense of disconnect in the possibility that this could even be considered? This process of subverting the very ideal of the American ideal of freedom is facilitated by a tenuous capacity for collective empathy, and perhaps also by the fact that the intended targets are non-citizens.

In my practice I have found that group therapy can be a powerful corrective for narcissism, particularly the absence of empathy or even curiosity, because the other is experienced as no more than an extension of the self. Evelyn, a group member who has generally felt angry at and victimized by men, explodes at Ed, another group member, whom she is convinced has insulted her. As the two of them and the rest of the group process this over time, I begin to notice an unfamiliar expression of curiosity on Evelyn's face. Recently, she has told me with genuine surprise, "He's just another human being, another person." How often do we therapists consider that this obliviousness and lack of empathy are not just about individual history and pathology, but are partly grounded in a larger societal narcissism?

> Maria complains that Ron is whiny and passive. Recently, he has become more open in group about his tendency to be passive and to withdraw. She says "The only thing that matters is to take action, otherwise I have no use for you. You're a loser." Diane says to Maria, "I don't like your dismissiveness." Diane had a dismissive, sarcastic, cold father. She's working on her own self-hatred. Her father lives on as an inner voice that attacks and criticizes her, and vividly imagines her cutting herself when she falls short of its standards. Their presentation is very different. Maria expresses contempt for others and appears to lack empathy for their vulnerabilities while Diane expresses self-contempt and lacks compassion for her own "weaknesses." Underneath they both share the same contempt and lack of empathy for the vulnerability that accompanies a need to connect with others.

Perhaps what is true for Maria and Diane holds true on a much larger scale. I wonder whether there hasn't been a rising incidence of Narcissistic Personality Disorder in this country over time, with its accompanying symptoms of pseudo-independence, deprivation, emptiness, alienation, restlessness, entitlement, envy, drivenness, etc. and whether there isn't a higher concentration in the US compared with those societies that are more firmly grounded in the ideal of community. Perhaps Diane and Maria mirror the larger society's over reliance on "can do" independence as a cover up for fear, hatred of helplessness, need and dependency, and an avoidance of collective empathy and responsibility, all part of acknowledging attachment.

In the process of writing this paper, I have come to believe that the psychic tensions I have described and many that I haven't addressed are universal. However, each person and each country finds their own particular balance on the continuum, a balance that we then label the *American Character,* uniquely distinct in some ways from the Canadian or French characters. It is as if we humans were hard wired to engage in communal research into the ancient Socratic question—what is the best way to live? And each country, like each individual then comes to their own version of the answer.

Writing this paper has also made me acutely aware of my own powerful temptation to argue a point, to get caught up in facts and figures, and bogged down in the battle of belief systems. This then, is my tentative, personal response to the question I posed at the beginning of this paper. What does this process of polarization distract me from? However frustrating the wheel-spinning impotence of blaming and externalizing, it feels easier than holding the complexity and ambiguity of my own grandiosity versus helplessness; of idealization of independence and freedom versus the vulnerability of my dependence on others; of my own "specialness" versus inconsequence; of my wish to trust versus my fear; of my sense that the world is ok with enough to go around, versus my sense of deprivation and anxious competitiveness in an unfriendly world.

I assume that we psychotherapists all share some version of these contradictions, some version of what abides in the American psyche. Since, as Phillips (1997) writes, "the analyst is an expert...in the forms ignorance can take in the service of self protection" and "psychoanalytic theory is a theory of the unbearable, of what one prefers not to know," it seems to me that we are in a powerful position to bear witness to and speak to those parts of ourselves and of the national psyche that we prefer not to know (p. 5, 13). I believe that our purpose and responsibility remain, as Freud originally wrote, to help make the unconscious conscious and that we fail to do so at our psychological, moral, spiritual and even physical peril.

Other than Gatsby, I can't imagine a more apt symbol for everything I have written than Superman. Superman has super powers, rescues people, acts on behalf of weak humanity, but shows little vulnerability or need for others, and crumples, like the fragile ideal he stands for, in the presence of kryptonite. The humanity is left to Clark Kent who doesn't hide his longing for Lois Lane, his sensitivity or his shrinking from life. No going after the "green light" for him. And it is hard to separate American identity from the pursuit of that magical green light of individual freedom, optimism and happiness that Gatsby so powerfully represents. What Nick says about Gatsby, might just as easily apply to America itself. "There was something gorgeous about him, some heightened sensitivity to the promises of life...an extraordinary gift for hope, a romantic readiness." Is there no middle way? Since psychotherapy helps us remember what we've "forgotten," helps us consciously include what we hate and deny in ourselves, to the extent that we can do this, perhaps we will discover our real heroes. May I suggest Christopher Reeves and his wife, Dana? ▼

References

Brooks, D. (9/10/2006). Of human bonding. *New York Times.*

Edsall, T. (2006). *Building red America: the new conservative coalition and the drive for permanent power.* New York, NY: Basic Books.

Fitzgerald, F.S. (1925). *The Great Gatsby.* New York, NY: Charles Scribner's Sons.

Kopp, S. (1976). *No hidden meanings: an illustrated eschatological laundry list.* Palo Alto, CA: Science and Behavior Books.

Phillips, A. (1997). *Terrors and experts.* London: Faber and Faber.

* * *

Commentary

MS. ENGELS'S CRITIQUE FROM A DECADE AGO SHOULD BE READ. AGAIN. "Now more than ever," as suggested in another era about the candidate Nixon. Think of this piece as an antidote to our current condition because of its depth, but also because of the non-reactive nature of reading it—the process of meditating on a *Voices* article as the ultimate un-Twitter act.

Between its original publication and this moment, the abiding American character Engels describes has found both healthy and unhealthy expressions. The empowering, healthy form was embodied by Barack Obama, arguably a narcissist, but self-aware and possessing great compassion (and chutzpah), willing even to sing "Amazing Grace" in the pulpit at a memorial service for the victims of a domestic terrorist attack.

The unhealthy nationalist form is now embodied by Donald Trump, a narcissist with neither grace nor compassion (but plenty of chutzpah), whose preoccupation appears to be aggrandizing himself in the eyes of others, and whose political genius is in finding and celebrating the lowest of the most common denominators.

All that aside, what's most exceptional about this article is that the essayist dares to step outside the individual frame to try to explain such things as culture and "socio-political contradictions." She ventures beyond the familiar comforts of the intrapsychic and interpersonal and this in a journal devoted to therapy and the therapy experience, mostly of individuals.

Engels's article, by my estimate, was a somber presage of the worst to come in American political and cultural life, and even the attempts of this journal to catch up in investigating it all. Now more than ever I think discovering the interface between knowledge of the individual and knowledge of larger group forces is needed. Engels ably accomplishes that here.

—Tom Burns, PhD

* * *

I APPLAUD THE AUTHOR'S EFFORTS TO BRING HER INSIGHTS AS A PSYCHOTHERAPIST TO A DEEPER UNDERSTANDING OF CHARACTER AS IT APPLIES TO OUR NATIONAL IDENTITY, as well as her appeal to us not to ignore this powerful context and its effect on our individual psyches. I would add that our understanding of what the process of individual growth looks like in psychotherapy can also shed light on how we interpret and respond to what is happening in our country now. The personal is political. Her article is even more prescient because it was written 12 years ago, before we had any idea about the degree to which the issues she raises would escalate. The difference is that now the veneer of denial about what we as a nation have disowned, projected, and defended against knowing about ourselves has been heavily confronted and exposed, like a raw nerve, the lace curtain of our "City on a Hill" torn.

In a paradoxical twist, this president's scorched earth approach to "draining the swamp," and "making America great again," may indeed be working—just not in the way he intended. Like a fly in the ointment of our idealized image, Trumpism has bulldozed into conscious awareness what has been lying just below the surface for a very long time and forced us to look squarely into the mirror. Isn't that, in large part, what psychotherapy is about? In a brilliant essay published in a recent issue of *Time*, Princeton Professor Eddie Glaude, Jr. (2018) says:

> ...we believed that our country had become less racist because we were not as brazen as we once were. Trump has shattered that illusion. ...But Trump isn't some nefarious character unlike anything we have seen before. He embodies the hatreds and fears that have been part of America's politics since its founding, and that erupt with every rapid change in our society and world. ...We must confront ourselves. ...What has for so long been hidden—or willfully ignored—is now in the open.

In our naiveté and denial, we thought we had largely achieved gender equality, until the #MeToo movement exposed the darker truth of ongoing male privilege and abuse of power. We took pride in thinking of ourselves as a land of freedom and refuge to "the huddled masses yearning to breathe free," until terms like "rapists," "mongrels," and "wall" began to surface in our discourse. By electing a Black president we congratulated ourselves on living in a post-racist society, until the Black Lives Matter movement exposed the illusion for what it was.

As the author suggests, I believe what is happening on our national stage, messy and painful as it is, like any confrontation of character, is part of a larger and necessary process. The practice of psychotherapy puts us in a unique position to have understandings about the process of character change and the loosening of self-defeating defensive postures as we see it revealed in the work we do on ourselves and with our patients. As we know, it is often arduous work, characterized by periods of risk and growth followed by reactive regressions when our anxiety about change overwhelms our capacity to cope. Often we must circle back around to re-work previous material we thought we had resolved. Why wouldn't the same be true of our collective?

I recently had the experience of talking politics with two sibling male cousins that I had not seen in decades. Though blood kin, the history and trajectory of our lives and our political leanings could not be more different. They identify strongly as devout Christians. One a career military man, the other a very successful business man, both have done exemplary things in their lives. They both spoke in reverential terms about Donald Trump, saying, "God sent him to us just in time." I swallowed hard.

Having just read Jonathan Haidt's (2012) *The Righteous Mind: Why Good People Are Divided by Politics and Religion*, and repeating Alex Redmountain's mantra, "less judgement, more curiosity," I vowed to listen with a curious and open mind. My aggressive and defensive judgment softened as I recalled the kind of childhood these men endured, growing up with their father, a hopeless alcoholic. At the tender ages of 10 and 12, they were physically restraining their father, who had shown up in a drunken rage, about to bash their sweet mother's head in with a railroad tie. Their boyhoods were chaotic and hellish. There was no Father, no protection, only poverty, humiliation, and terror. Longing for order, safety, and protection where there was none, I can see how these men would be vulnerable to projecting those needs onto the "fatherly" sounding Trumpian message, which taps into the illusion of what good fathering promises to offer. Despite the profound irony that this White House is described by many as "chaotic," and "off the rails," the seductive illusion of protection, restoration of order, and safety for their way of life speaks to their trauma. With the understanding my work as a therapist affords me, I can access some compassion for their vulnerability and allegiance. In some ways, it feels to me as though we are all living in that chaotic alcoholic home with them. During times of turmoil and uncertainty, most of us want some degree of safety and protection. It's just that we differ on what that looks like. And, though coming at it from a very different place informed by my faith in human process, I might even agree with my cousins that the arc of human history suggests the Trump presidency came "just in time."

As in any effective psychotherapy, armed with emerging awareness, we come to a crossroads where we must decide what kind of person and, in parallel process, what kind of country we want to be. Eddie Glaude could as easily be describing the process of psychotherapy as our social and political process: "Forward movement is halting, inhibited, interrupted. Our history, if we're honest, suggests we will fail. No matter. We go on—together."

—Dairlyn Chelette, LCSW

References:

Glaude, Jr., E. (2018, September 17). Don't let the loud bigots distract you. America's real problem with race cuts far deeper. *Time, 192* (11). Retrieved online at http://time.com/5388356/our-racist-soul/

Haidt, J. (2012). *The righteous mind: Why good people are divided by politics and religion.* New York: Pantheon Books.

▼

Some people are born on third base and go through life thinking they hit a triple.

—Unknown, attributed to Barry Switzer

Cathy Roberts

Friendships Lost and Found:
Racial Oppression and Emerging Freedom

CATHY ROBERTS, LCPC, counsels individuals and couples in Rockville, Maryland. A racial equity educator, she presents workshops nationally and is adjunct faculty at the University of Maryland School of Social Work. Freeing herself from tendencies to oppress and be oppressed is her core life work. For fun, she travels abroad and hangs out at home with grandchildren, Link, Kyra, and Pax, three amazing beings with whom she shares abundant love, laughter, and play. *cathy@cathyroberts.net*

If you have come here to help me, you are wasting your time. But if you have come because your liberation is bound up with mine, then let us work together.

—Lilla Watson

Part I: 1968 Bound Up

//Why are you friends with Alice?" sneered my sixth grade classmate as we played outside in the schoolyard. "She smells bad and she doesn't shave her armpits!" I froze. My day had started off with such promise. I wore my new pink flowered suit, a knee length skirt and blazer affair with a lacy white shell underneath. Totally mod go-go boots on my size 9 feet completed my ensemble. I felt halfway grown up. Then came the verbal attack aimed at me and at Alice, who stood a few feet away, watching.

Alice was the first African American student to integrate our close knit class in my small public elementary school in Silver Spring, Maryland. Just emerging from sundown town status, the housing codes prohibiting African Americans from buying and renting housing in this DC suburb were loosening. In 2018, one of the few places in the United States where being Black and male doesn't negatively impact social status and upward mobility (Badger, Cain Miller, Pearce, and Quealy, 2018), it was a different suburb in the 1960's. Back then the only African Americans I saw were men collecting the garbage from the clanging metal cans in our tidy back yard and the handful of women cooking dinner at the homes of a few friends from families of greater wealth and different values than mine.

I took to Alice immediately. Tall and skinny like me, we were Twiggy in Black and White. I visited her house, met her father—the first Black man I saw wearing a suit—and started a friendship. We were athletic, neighbors, and seemingly a good fit—until the schoolyard confrontation and my response to it drove a wedge between us. As Alice met my eyes, I was filled with a shame my 11-year-old brain did not understand. Nothing in childhood equipped me to stand up for Alice and our friendship. Could I be friends with her and with the pack of White friends I'd known since Kindergarten? If that was possible, I did not know how to navigate the territory. While my parents had encouraged me to be kind towards and respectful of everyone, they were not pioneers in equity. They lacked the skills to acknowledge and communicate difficult feelings, hardships, and challenges. I don't recall sharing this incident with them. By age 11, I had learned to keep much to myself to ward off further humiliation from parents embarrassed by my feelings of fear, shame, and anger. My humanity was not especially welcome in my childhood home. Fearing more chastisement at school, I unfriended Alice. I don't recall the details of how this went. I don't think Alice and I talked about it. I certainly didn't have the skills to do that. Looking back, I think my shame was the feeling that I had done something wrong by being friends with Alice in the first place, and that maybe I deserved the taunts of the White friend. With this experience, I was harshly initiated into a new world where I no longer felt safe. My friendship with Alice jeopardized my friendships with White kids. My White friends were playing a game I'd never known before. The "prove you're White enough to be our friend" game had unwritten rules and I needed to figure them out, or I would lose my status in White world. It would take nearly 50 years for me to remember this encounter and question what really happened in those few second so very long ago.

Part II: 2018 Emerging Liberation

The afternoon sun shines on Button Farm, a living history agricultural preserve 20 miles north of Washington, DC. We are gathered for a group celebration of Juneteenth, the day enslaved Texans learned they were free, two and a half years after the Emancipation Proclamation. The afternoon is coming to an end, and I don't want to leave the farm. Together we led a circle dialogue about what it means to be free, how we want to lean in to more freedom, and what gets in our way. We shared with people we know and with complete strangers. We moseyed through the fields to visit an old, old, slave cemetery—so old the symbols on the stones are African. We communed with our own ancestors as well as those buried for hundreds of years beneath our feet.

People drift toward their cars. I linger, wanting more company and companionship with my friends and colleagues from Coming to the Table (CTTT), an organization with a mission of racial reconciliation. As I tarry, I am aware of feeling deep comfort and connection in this place, with these particular people. I am also aware that in this group, I am the only White person present. The four friends are African American and south Asian. Although I've spent my entire life within 15 miles of my birthplace, I consider how far I have traveled inside myself to arrive at this place where I feel this much enjoyment and ease being in a racially diverse group. Until recently, I wasn't aware of the pressure to play by White rules—rules that have lived in me since I was born and became cemented that spring day 50 years ago when I was directly confronted with racism. Until recently, my training in White superiority was invisible to me, drilled down deep in my bones. I've spent years now working to free myself from that training. As I free myself, a journey which I expect to last a lifetime, I have much appreciation for and enjoyment with the very people I was taught to secretly consider inferior.

Part III: 1968-2018 The Journey

Spotty relationships with African Americans and anyone who was not White followed my elementary school playground experience. I walked home from junior high school with African American girls, Lisa and Vanessa, but had no African American friends in high school, though I had a mini crush on Lamar, whom I admired for his artistic abilities. I avoided anyone who didn't look like me in college. Fifteen years later, adopting my daughter, whose biological parents were from Cambodia, I did all the right things. We attended the spring New Year at the Buddhist Temple, took the family to the Pacific Asian American Festival at Freedom Plaza, served jasmine rice, made friends with Asian families. I still didn't get it though. I still didn't understand what I had that my daughter didn't: the privilege of White skin and European ancestry. That lack of acknowledgement created problems and barriers for me that I was unconscious of. Until I wasn't.

Two encounters with African American women stand out from the pre-conscious era. One occurred at my counseling internship and the other at a women's conference. I don't remember the lead up to either. I do recall the unpleasant, even nasty, tone with which the women addressed me. I wish I could travel back through time and review these scenes with my 2018 eyes. My guess is that I committed some micro-aggression in either my speech or manner that negatively impacted the women. Micro-aggression was not even a word in my vocabulary in the early 2000's. I had yet to awaken to my privileged state. In the underbelly of that ignorance, I suspect that I harmed without meaning to and without knowing it. I still make microaggressions. The difference now is that I am open to hearing about what I said or did and to making amends. This creates a different sort of openness in my relationships with African Americans, as well as other people of color.

As I reflect on how I've traveled from unfriending Alice to wanting more with my CTTT friends that warm June afternoon at Button Farm, I recall moments of waking up along the way. The first glimpse of awakening happened while I stood in line at a second hand store. Noticing I was taller and White and other shoppers were shorter and Brown, I actually *felt* my privilege consciously for the first time. Pride at my height and White skin coursed through my body, and I stood a little taller—for a nanosecond. As soon as that pride was conscious, I was repulsed. How could I feel better about myself at the expense of Brown people around me? I now know my response was a learned family and societal pattern going back generations. In that moment, the implicit became explicit. I saw myself and disliked what I saw. I buried my discovery for several years.

A second wake up moment happened as I literally awoke from sleep one December morning. "How did slavery hurt me?" I wondered. Third great-granddaughter of enslavers on both sides of my family, I dug into the truth about my family's trauma and my own. Not in any way diminishing the trauma of enslaved people and their descendants, I grappled with emerging awareness that *oppressive systems diminish the humanity of everyone.* This jolt of awareness propelled me with greater strength than my Trader Joe's Irish Breakfast tea to look at my role in perpetuating and perpetrating racism. The learned compulsivity of my White youth set the stage for me to focus on racism in the United States. I absorbed everything I could about the history, culture, and systemic racism that pervades every institution in the country. The knowledge I gained and experiences I had researching racial equity took me into spaces where I was one of a few White people. I attended events about racism in Maryland and across the country. I taught graduate students and made friends with African Americans ages 24-80. I found myself welcomed into Black spaces, invited to churches and meals, and most importantly, accepted for being a curious, fallible, White woman.

The oppressive nature of White supremacy is knit deeply into my bones, and I still make microaggressions. My intention may be genuine and authentic, but the impact is hurtful. I expect to make mistakes. I think I always will because there is so much of my racial identity and cultural racism that remains invisible to me. Sometimes I feel embarrassed, as when I recently said in front of about 50 people that I could take a break from countering a racist act, and a kind African American woman pointed out that my privilege was speaking. She reminded me that she hasn't the luxury of taking such a break. I felt abashed when I assumed all the participants in the workshop I was facilitating were White based on their appearance. An Iranian woman and a Latina woman gradually let me know they were present. I stumbled into discomfort with my own sweet CTTT group before the Juneteenth event when, frustrated at the time and energy we put into our gatherings while attracting few attendees, I blurted out, "I'm ready to find a White person to take my place!" One of my Black colleagues asked me what I meant, giving me space to explain that CTTT tradition encourages co-facilitators, one of African and one of European descent. He accepted my explanation. I still felt awkward and revisited my blurted comment. He said that once I explained it, he got it. And yes, my privilege was showing in my comment, he went on, before kindly saying, "you're our very own entitled White person" in such a loving way that I felt seen, claimed, and accepted. Knowing that I will make mistakes and people will take offense helps me to open myself to the feedback I get from those I have offended. Conversations provide an opportunity to make amends. I find that sometimes, but not always, this simple but not easy process brings us closer.

At this point in my racial recovery, I know that my liberation is bound up with that of all people. My skin is thinner when it comes to empathy and thicker when people disparage me for my beliefs. I show up differently wherever I go. I like to fantasize that I'm back in that 1968 school yard with my childhood friend taunting Alice and me. I hear the jeer about Alice and her body odor and unshaved underarms. I look my White friend straight in the eyes and maintain eye contact as I say, "So what!" And keep eye contact until something else happens. I don't know what. And Alice would see that I am with her. ▼

References:

Badger, E., Cain Miller, C., Pearce, A., & Quealy, K. (2018, March 19). "Extensive data shows punishing reach of racism for Black boys". *The New York Times,* retrieved online at https://www.nytimes.com/interactive/2018/03/19/upshot/race-class-white-and-black-men.html

Lisa Kays

Voices in the Classroom:
Teaching Diversity is Not a Job for One

LISA KAYS is a White, straight, cis clinical social worker in private practice in Washington DC, where she works with individuals, couples and groups. In addition to traditional psychotherapy, her professional adventures include the integration of improv with therapy, and her Improv for Therapists classes have been featured on *NBC4* and in *The Washington Post*. She has also recently delved into teaching diversity at the MSW level and is increasingly interested in doing work around themes of race, diversity, privilege and oppression. She lives in Washington, DC with her husband and young son, all of whom are awaiting the arrival of their newest family addition this winter.
LISA@LISAKAYS.COM

Can a straight, White woman teach diversity effectively? Should she?

"Sure!" I rationalized to myself when I was asked to be an adjunct professor within a social work program's course on diversity in a multicultural society in the spring of 2016. Teaching this course, I thought, could not come at a better time. It felt like a vehicle to foster and model the tolerance, empathy, and ability to hold conflicting opinions that I so wanted to see throughout the country, while also helping inform and educate people about social justice and systemic oppression. I had felt powerless politically and socially for much of 2015 and 2016, and this finally felt like a way to do something, even if on a small scale.

Was there doubt that it was appropriate for a straight White woman to teach this course? Yes. Were there not social workers of color, I wondered? Gay social workers? Activist social workers, even, or those working for longer and with more vulnerable populations than I, who were therefore more qualified to do this? Nah, I told myself. It's fine. I'm a woman, and women are oppressed. And plus, I'm woke. (Strike one.)

Getting Started

I had just published a piece in the "Race & Racism" issue of *Voices*. And I remembered Alicia Sanchez Gil's article about how alienated she had felt as a Black woman in her diversity course.

I decided to use her essay to open the class. Alicia's words helped students to say with relief, "I was scared I was going to have to be the voice of all Black people in this class, too."

I credit the essay with setting a safe, curious, open tone for both semesters I taught.

The first semester, students were so affected by her essay that some of them Google-stalked her.

"You know she went to the school you graduated from, right?"

"I'm sorry, what?"

Hello, White privilege! I had assumed that this was impossible, that my school, based on my own experience in it, had been a place that felt safe and welcoming for everyone. With one fact, my students proved otherwise, and made an important point, unknowingly, about how blind privilege can be. I reached out to a former classmate. "Did you feel safe in our MSW classes as a Black student?"

"Of course not," she said. "It was awful. Everyone always turned to me and the other Black student to answer questions about being Black, like we were spokespeople."

"I'm so sorry. Why didn't I know?"

"How could you?" she said. "You couldn't have seen it."

Her compassion was as genuine as my privilege was blind. Not only did I not see it, but there was no expectation that I could.

I thought more about how to frame the class. When I took the course, we had a number of guest speakers representing oppressed groups, but Alicia's essay and the current political and social climate told me that wasn't the right approach.

I heard Alicia when she wrote, "I could ... speak up, constantly in the teaching role as the token person of color speaking on behalf of all people of color..." (2016, p. 35). Other activist writers argue against the oppressed doing the emotional labor of educating the oppressor about their oppression (Collins, 2010).

So I would invite speakers not to address their status as oppressed people, but their process of realizing and owning their own privilege and working to address it in society.

I was still mulling over options when I got a message from Michael Giordano, who (with Sean LeSane, Cathy Roberts, and Gil Bliss) had guest-edited the "Race & Racism" issue: "Sean and I heard you're using the *Voices* issue in your class. We're available to come speak."

I was delighted. I had wanted to invite them originally, but in keeping with my concerns about asking the oppressed to educate others, I didn't want to ask a Black man and a gay man to come speak. But, if they were offering, that felt different.

We held this panel twice, once in the fall and once in the spring semester classes. In preparation, the students had already read Alicia's article. I asked them to read Michael and Sean's essay in the previous issue of *Voices* on their inter-racial friendship and to pick one other essay from the "Race & Racism" issue to read.

Alicia, Michael and Sean were vulnerable, candid, honest and wise. The students asked challenging personal and professional questions and pulled them aside afterwards to ask more. Much of the student writing and discussion later would center around the impact these individuals had on them.

Why Me?

But perhaps the greatest impact was on me. I had rationalized teaching the course as a White woman. Alicia, Michael, and Sean's presence in the classroom made that harder to do.

Sean and Michael spoke with more authority and experience about marginalization and oppression from the perspective of being Black and gay than I could, even though I was a woman with my own experience of oppression. Some of it was surely because I was the instructor and they were more candid as guest speakers, but that wasn't the whole story.

I noticed how quickly Alicia was able to identify power dynamics in the classroom and within the discourse that were problematic and that I had missed completely or couldn't name effectively. When the class began to wonder if those in subordinate groups weren't heard because they are too angry or not polite enough when they speak, for instance, Alicia described the concept of "tone policing." Strike two: blatantly missing obvious power imbalances or aspects of systemic oppression in the classroom.

Alicia was better equipped to teach this class and to help the students see what they needed to see. She was also more qualified. Her expertise and career are focused on macro, systemic issues of social justice. Why isn't Alicia teaching this class? I started to wonder to myself. Why me?

Teaching Oppression

Now I feel the way Alicia describes in her *Voices* piece. Are the people who hired me going to hate me for saying this? Will they feel betrayed? Is this fair to say? I value my relationships with the school and the people who hired me. They are, as Alicia comments below, "nice and well-meaning White people." They are good, ethical, social workers committed to social justice.

But, I note, we are all White. Is this a blind spot? Perhaps I had landed where I was due to the White equivalent of the "old boys' network," not because people were trying to discriminate or be unfair, but because unconscious bias is just that, unconscious.

I question how diversity is taught, which is not unique to the school where I teach. The MSW curriculum is standardized nationally, and I imagine that social work diversity courses mirror similar programs in psychology and counseling. Teaching diversity has led me to wonder about the following possible changes.

Team Teaching

Diversity could be team-taught by two people representing different positions in the dominant/subordinate position. Dialogue groups, as presented in my students' textbook, "are co-led by trained facilitators who belong to participating social identity groups" (Zuniga, 2010, p. 635). Co-taught by Alicia and me, for instance, or Michael and Alicia, etc., the class could give students two leaders to project their questions and idealizations and doubts onto.

The need for this became powerfully evident to me when, in a class session after the *Voices* panel, the students expressed concern at how "angry" and "aggressive" Alicia was. I did my best to facilitate this discussion, focusing the class back on tone-policing and our reading about how often Black women who are opinionated, differ with the status quo, or assert themselves, are known as "angry Black women." I reminded the class about Alicia herself writing about this fear in her essay and discussing it in class. I asked for specific ways her behavior was aggressive according to a concrete definition. "Would you feel differently if she were a White man?" I asked, to uncomfortable silence. Despite my attempts, the conversation remained muddied and unclear. It was unfinished. Alicia wasn't there do to the "working through." I could attempt to speak on her behalf and explain what I thought she meant or felt, but it wasn't the same because I am not her. My voice was an important one to have with hers in this class dynamic. Would the question have been raised at all if we were co-teaching? How would the relationship between her and the students who feared her aggression have played out over time? What would have been gained or lost in that?

Class Format

Diversity class is generally taught as a combination of lecture, reading, and some discussion. As a group therapist, I find this limiting, as the skills I think are most critical to the therapist are:
  a) the ability to accept one's privilege,
  b) the ability to see and acknowledge the oppression of others, and
  c) the ability to incorporate both into meaningful dialogue and change with other individuals, groups, and communities.

In my experience, the best way to teach these skills is through group process, which facilitates the following:
  a) spotting and addressing uncomfortable feelings or power imbalances in the moment,
  b) skills to slow down and examine an issue or conflict with decreasing defensiveness and shame and increased compassion and curiosity, and
  c) depth, intimacy, and genuine learning through honest questioning and dialogue around "stupid questions" that need to be asked and answered for true understanding.

In one class, a White student respectfully asked one student of color to participate more so she could benefit from his experience. The Black student replied, in essence, "I don't always want to, and I don't have to." In a process group model, the White student would have more space to speak about her longing for more participation from the Black students, what that's like and what's behind it, and what it's like to be refused. Questions about entitlement to that information from Black or other minority students could be explored. Black students would be free to question what it's like to be asked and to refuse; to notice if they wanted to connect more and felt held back by a difference in power. A rich exchange between and among students could occur.

Another powerful example of group process happened when the class split into groups to work on an assignment about race. One group happened to have three White students, and a Black student said he would join them. A White student said to him reflexively, "Are you sure you'll be comfortable? I don't want you to feel weird."

Confused, the Black student said, "No, why would I be uncomfortable?"

I asked the two if we could discuss this interaction in connection with the dynamics we were studying in class. They were open to it, and we proceeded to explore and better understand how the White student had projected her discomfort with having the Black student in the group while doing an assignment exploring colorblindness and the discomfort White people feel in discussing race in mixed groups.

The Black student, because we were having a process around it, was then able to say, "This happens all the time to me. White people are constantly saying, 'Are you okay

with this?' or apologizing if I'm the only Black guy, and I never get why. I'm fine with it."
The other Black students in the class nodded in agreement.

"So you are often asked to carry the anxiety of White people about their own racism or racial dynamics in this society?" I asked. That question opened some eyes. Group process did that, and I believe it's critical to any meaningful learning about difference, equality, domination and subordination.

In Vivo Examples

Another way that I've introduced group process is by offering extra credit to students who call out microaggressions in class. Microaggressions are "the everyday verbal, non-verbal, and environmental slights, snubs, or insults, whether intentional or unintentional, that communicate hostile, derogatory, or negative messages to target persons based solely on their marginalized group membership" (Sue, 2010, p. 3). I wanted to make sure students understood experientially what a micro-aggression was.

I also think this is one of the most important social justice tools we have and the hardest to use. Who, in a meeting with co-workers and their boss, wants to say, "Excuse me, but you just made an uncomfortable generalization when you said 'Hey, guys,' given that this is a mixed-gender group," or, "It may not be comfortable for everyone to be in a workplace that only honors Christian holidays." The classroom could be a space to practice this, and the extra credit sent the message that it would be rewarded, not punished. While this doesn't mirror the real world, it encouraged acts of bravery and perhaps allowed the psychological experience of calling out micro-aggression to be positive.

It was shocking, quite frankly, to note how many microaggressions they caught that I didn't notice. Not to mention how many I made. Some I did and waited patiently for a student to note them, but a few slipped by me. (Strike three, if you're keeping score.)

A few examples of microaggressions called out in the class in 2018 included those against "people from West Virginia" (classist micro-aggression), "Trump supporters" (classist micro-aggression, given the context), "colored people," "White people," women being interrupted by men, and ageist microaggressions towards both younger and older people.

In my experience, there is more to be gained from these conversations than from reading about theoretical concepts of oppression and systems of injustice. As a teacher, I have seen that our defenses against acknowledging oppression are far stronger than a textbook, but, perhaps, not strong enough to battle personal relationship and connection.

Course Name and Content

"Why isn't this class called 'Oppression?'" Alicia asked numerous times. First, I thought, "Because we are talking about the experiences of different groups." Now though, as I teach and learn, I realize that what binds those experiences is whether a status is oppressed or not. The systemic oppression of gay individuals in our society happens in much the same way as that of the poor and of Muslims. So why not focus on those mechanisms rather than on the experiences of different groups?

A traditional diversity approach is to learn about groups we don't know much about in isolation. Allan G. Johnson (2010) writes in the textbook for the class,

Taking responsibility means not waiting for others to tell you what to do, to point out what's going on, or to identify alternatives. If dominant groups are going to take their share of responsibility, it's up to them to listen, watch, ask, and listen again, to make it their business to find out for themselves (p. 614).

Placing this responsibility on students, rather than making diversity class a "parade of oppressed groups," requires students to learn about different groups as they become relevant in their work and teaches them how to do such learning—which should be the focus of the class. Not to study gay people, but to learn what are the appropriate materials, points of view, and factors to look at, so that as students encounter different people and oppressed groups throughout their careers, they know how to do this. This also prevents students from spending time learning about a group they belong to, which addresses Alicia's concern about diversity classes being geared, however unintentionally, to teaching privileged White students about the Other.

It's my responsibility, if I take seriously what I teach, to wonder and think aloud, and even have this read by those whom I fear I may offend. If I invite my students to ask themselves hard questions and to serve as allies and speak truth to power, I must also do that work, even when I am unsure. If Alicia can hit "send" when she is scared, so, surely, must I, for as long as the system is structured as it is, she will always have far more to lose.

I will continue to reflect on this, although I am not currently teaching, bolstered by the ideas and connections I've made through *Voices* and how it has been woven so meaningfully into the classroom in ways I didn't imagine when I included Alicia's essay in the first class.

As a means of taking responsibility, I wrote Alicia and said, if asked to teach again, I'd like to propose that she teach with me if she wanted to. Or, I offered, if she'd rather teach it alone, I would recommend that instead. Adjuncts do not staff a university program. But I can make recommendations and ask for new terms if I notice a system isn't serving social justice as well as it could be.

My clinical supervisor reminds me to work with the relationships directly in reach. "Lisa," she says, "we change the world one relationship at a time." ▼

* * *

Commentary

IMAGINE MY SURPRISE WHEN SOMEONE REACHED OUT TO ME: "I read your article from the *Voices* journal in class, and I wanted you to know that it really resonated with me—I am citing it in my own work." I flashed back to the moment I pressed "send" on my article, "Diversity from Within." I was awash with panic. I questioned everything. Was I too candid? Not candid enough? I didn't use any data—would people minimize my experience without it? Would all the nice and well-meaning White people be really mad at me? Would I be black-listed (pun intended) from all social work gatherings from this moment on?

Learning that my work was read in a real-life social work class shifted my relationship to my own writing. What began as a daunting and scary process became a liberating tool for solidarity. Knowing that one student felt less alone after reading my words was impactful. Knowing that my experience may have shifted the conversation about addressing oppression in the field from the inside out was profound.

—Alicia Sanchez Gil

References

Collins, P. H. (2010). Toward a new vision: Race, class, and gender. *Readings for Diversity and Social Justice* (3rd ed.), 606-611.

Johnson, A. (2010). What can we do? *Readings for Diversity and Social Justice* (3rd ed.), 612-618.

Sanchez Gil, A. (2016). *Short report:* Diversity from within. *Voices: The Art and Science of Psychotherapy. 52* (3), 35-37.

Sue, D. W. (Ed.) (2010). Microaggressions, marginality and oppression: An introduction. *Microaggressions and Marginality: Manifestations, Dynamic and Impact.* John Wiley & Sons: Hoboken, New Jersey.

Zuniga, X. (2010). Bridging differences through dialogue. *Readings for Diversity and Social Justice* (3rd ed.), 635-638.

Kyriarchy: defined in feminist theory as a social system built around domination, oppression, and submission, extending patriarchy beyond gender to encompass and connect to other structures of oppression and privilege, such as racism, ableism, capitalism, etc.

—coined by Elisabeth Schussler Fiorenza,
feminist scholar of liberation theology, 1992

Susan McClure

Turning Purple

We have met the enemy...and he is US.

—Pogo

ONTHS BEFORE THE 2008 PRESIDENTIAL ELEC-
TION TOOK PLACE, I STOOD IN FRONT OF THE
TV IN TEARS as candidate Obama talked about
his vision of America no longer being a society of red and
blue states, but of an electorate that embraced the larger
definition of an America that had become purple. At the
time I wanted to believe it was possible that red and blue
could be blended into purple and that this Black man
could be the agent of that transformation. But I should
have known better: Change usually happens when the
pendulum swings from one end to the other before moving slowly toward the middle. We may yet make it to purple, but from my own personal experience, that isn't going
to happen any time soon. For now, the division between
red and blue seems to be getting worse. This collision of
opposites is showing us how polarized we are as a nation,
with one another, and within ourselves.

The peninsula of Charleston, SC, where I have practiced for 35 years, is evenly divided between Democrats
and Republicans, as is my practice. I realize this is not the
case for most of my friends who are psychotherapists, and
I have come to believe that the differences in our experiences may be largely a function of whom we relate to
day in and day out. A substantial segment of my patients
are in or have retired from the military; another segment
come from the Southern gentry, some of whom have families who are written about in history books both from
the time of the Revolutionary War and the Civil War.
The majority of them had been dissatisfied with Obama's

SUSAN MCCLURE, PHD, is a clinical
psychologist who has been in private practice in Charleston, South
Carolina, since 1983. Trained in
a variety of psychodynamic ap-
proaches, she blends dream work
with voice dialogue in her work
with individuals, partnerships, and
groups. Before becoming a psychologist, she worked as an urban
planner and community organizer
and edited a community monthly
magazine for 7 years; she continues
to keep her hand in those pursuits.
smcclure47@gmail.com

understated and conciliatory manner and seemed to celebrate Trump's comfort with strutting his wealth, power, and position in the world. The rest of my practice is composed of therapists, lawyers, artists, and entrepreneurs, most of whom were born other places and moved to Charleston because they chose to.

In the months before the 2016 election I noticed that more and more of the material from both conservative and liberal patients was oriented toward positions, opinions, and rants about candidates and what was happening in the political arena. I began to be concerned that the personal quality of our psychotherapy work was being subsumed by the energy of the collective. While I almost never comment on my own political opinions or identification in therapy, most of my patients correctly assessed that I was a Democrat and their views of me and interactions with me began to revolve around the way we were alike or different. A patient I will call Alan, a retired submarine captain, told me during the months before the election that he had hesitated talking about how poorly he felt the people in the armed forces were treated under the two previous Democratic administrations. He had tears in his eyes as he talked about the hardships his fellow submariners had faced. This experience affected me deeply as I recognized that in some way I didn't remember, I had communicated that I was not available to hear anything about Democratic incumbents.

Although I have always considered myself a Democrat, I could not support either Clinton or Sanders. During most of the pre-election season, as I watched the debates and a broad cross-section of news sources, I noticed that I was becoming less partisan. Simultaneously I developed a growing distaste for self-righteousness and disrespectful ways of presenting one's positions, which I felt were turning the election uglier and uglier.

Meanwhile, in my own practice, I continued to be faced with looking at all of the issues through each patient's eyes. I found I could find some value in both conservative and liberal positions. These people were making intellectual and ethical sense to me, although their backgrounds and points of view were in some ways quite different from mine. Many of them had been raised "South of Broad," which is where the families live whose last names can be found in history books. What disturbed me the most was the ease with which the red and blue clients projected their shadows onto one another and vilified the other. I had to move carefully in my sessions to avoid that happening between me and my patients.

Another thing happened: The longer this went on the more cautious and quiet I became. I was responding to the polarization by becoming more neutral, which was my first tip-off about what being purple might be like.

By the time I settled on a presidential candidate I could both personally admire and politically support, John Kasich, most of my friends and colleagues (Democrats) were distancing themselves from me. For them my purpleness was a betrayal of our relationship. How could I be their friend or colleague if I could see some value in the positions of their opponents? I was shocked and hurt by their reactions and felt devalued by their unwillingness to listen to the process by which I had come to my decision. After all, I believed I had arrived at my decisions as thoughtfully as they had. The toughest moment came when my closest friend since graduate school said my political stance had made it impossible for us to continue to be close. Given all we have shared and how deeply we understood one another, I was devastated that she seemed unable to trust me or my judgment.

The day after the results were counted I heard from several friends and colleagues who had been Clinton or Sanders supporters and who were in shock and outrage, incredulous that Trump had won. And I also listened to my patients, half of whom were ecstatic and half of whom were scared and upset, trying to make myself available to both as they processed their feelings about themselves and the country now. I didn't know how to deal with the results of the election, but I did understand that regardless of who had won, the polarization and oppositional way of relating had formed a deep chasm in my own relationships and in the lives of everyone I knew. That was the thing that scared me the most.

It is clear that our country is in the process of a chaotic and dramatic transformation which touches our personal and professional lives. Red and blue patients, friends and colleagues, all repeat to me their dreams about Trump, and sometimes I am invited to share with them fears of how they may be like him. For most of them it is appalling. For some it is exciting and promising.

A year and a half later while attending a process group at an AAP conference I found myself sharing this experience. As we discussed our reactions to the polarization of the country since the election, I volunteered that it had brought me to vote for John Kasich in the primary and shared how much it had cost me in friendships. I was surprised when one of the members leaned forward and said pointedly: "It is people like you who got Trump elected!" Her feelings were still raw. And my purpleness was definitely not ok. Another member came up to me during our group break and told me she never again would see me in the same way she had. Interestingly, I found I had become used to this kind of reaction. I do not take it personally anymore. I think most of us are scared about how bad things might get.

If I step back, the upheaval we are now experiencing seems to be part of our psychological, cultural, and political character, which at one point led to the Revolutionary and Civil wars. Perhaps we are again reworking what it means to be Americans. Perhaps we are still creating a nation in which there is room to transform red and blue into purple. But for now we are at war in fundamental ways that again threaten our sense of selves and our safety as individuals. No wonder we feel vulnerable. No wonder emotions are running so high. Regardless of where each of us is on the spectrum of red to blue and where our patients are on it, our task is the same, is it not? We are psychotherapists and as such have come to value and to be able to be present to what the OTHER thinks and feels and to understand that their vulnerabilities and defenses are affecting their lives as much as ours are. Perhaps from that place we can reunite as Americans someday. I doubt that will happen quickly, but our future as a country depends on it. Maybe we are a part of making that happen. ▼

John Wojnowski. 2018. Nicholas Kirsch

Nicholas Kirsch

Uses, Misuses, and Abuses of Power by Donald Trump, Me, and You

Nearly all men can stand adversity, but if you want to test a man's character, give him power.
—Abraham Lincoln

NICHOLAS KIRSCH, PhD, Washington, DC. His interest in power dynamics began in his family many years ago as his intelligent, well intended (therapist) parents kept misusing their power to the detriment of the family. He majored in government and interned on Capitol Hill, but, disheartened by the pervasive corruption, left politics for psychotherapy. He now helps individuals, groups, and organizations discover their full power potential without compromising integrity. He sees the world's current demise as a product of misused power and lack of integrity at all levels of society. He loves road biking, novels, hiking, and worrying about his young adult children.
nicholaskirsch56@gmail.com

WASHINGTON, DC, OUR COUNTRY'S POWER CAPITAL AND MY BELOVED HOME OF 60 YEARS, IS NOTHING IF NOT A CITY OF CONTRASTS AND CONTRADICTIONS. It is a city of the highest ideals and the worst corruption, where Barack Obama, the most progressive president of our generation, presided for 8 years followed immediately by our most autocratic and tyrannical president, Donald Trump. I'm privileged to live on Embassy Row, where my rat-infested alley is just a few blocks from Jeff Bezos' new $150 million mansion. I commute by bike each day past the opulent mansions built for 19th-century robber barons and captains of industry, now converted to embassies and luxury hotels. Passing the South African embassy, I pump my fist in solidarity with the bronze Nelson Mandela, his fist held high in defiance toward the statue of the stately imperialist Winston Churchill, standing smug across the way at Britain's embassy. Further up the hill, in front of the Vatican's embassy, a man named John Wojnowski stands meek but resolute, placard held high, "Vatican Hides Pedophiles." Sexually abused by his priest as a teenager, for 20 years he has doggedly shined the light on Vatican abuses and cover-ups. For the first 10-15 years of his solo protest he was pelted with tomatoes and stones, beaten, and mercilessly screamed at by Christian passersby; now he is cheered and waved at admiringly as a hero.

Finally I pass Sidwell Friends, the uber-progressive Quaker school for the children of DC's liberal elites

(Obamas, Gores, Bidens, Clintons, Merrick Garland, and my own ragtag Kirsch boys). Though an icon of progressive politics, Sidwell was the very last DC high school to admit Black students because one wealthy racist Quaker woman on the board vetoed them. In DC the symbols of power, its uses, misuses, and abuses abound.

Having power alters how we feel in our bodies, how we understand the world, and how we treat other people. The misuse and corruption of power have bedeviled the world since time immemorial. This is not new or unique to the Donald Trump era, though it may feel new to many "coastal progressives" who for a few generations have taken for granted the universal acceptance of their humanistic ideals. Part of what makes the use of power so bedeviling is that inherent in being a person with power (or authority) is the fact that decisions you make will hurt and be unfair to some people while favoring other people; and determining whether these hurtful decisions constitute abuse or corruption versus reasonable uses of power is highly subjective. The fact that someone is hurt or unfairly treated by a governing body does not inherently mean that power has been abused; it often is the unfortunate consequence or side effect of a just act. Because of this subjectivity, whether we're studying pedophile priests, 19th-century robber barons, racist Quakers, Jeff Bezos, psychotherapists, or Donald Trump, it is possible to justify almost any hurtful behavior as valid under the flag of needing to gain or consolidate power.

Instinctual Quest for Power

Human desire for power, and willingness to at times do most anything to attain or retain it, lies deep in our genetic programming, in the reptilian portion of our brain. Our basic survival instincts generate a drive for power, since having power over others helps ensure our protection, dominance and survival. Despite 50 million years of evolving our intellectual and emotional brains, the reptilian foundation persists in exerting its preeminence and causes humans to suspend moral principles and lose rational thinking and empathy. (This has been vividly demonstrated by many psychology experiments including the infamous Milgram electric-shock studies of the 1960s showing that empowered authority figures will lose their principles to the point of torturing others, and the 1971 Stanford Prison Experiment that had to be terminated prematurely when a group of students randomly assigned to role play prison guards over another group started actually abusing the second group.)

At a societal level this power-grabbing instinct of human nature is what leads to wars, genocides, slavery, torture, huge disparities in resource distribution, environmental devastation, etc. And at the individual behavioral level as in the case of Donald Trump and other persons in authority (including psychotherapists), it leads to lying, bullying, cheating, complacency, racism, misogyny, exclusivity, favoritism, and many other abuses/misuses of power.

Principles vs. Power

Listening closely to regular Trump supporters and not just his publicists at Fox News, the Alt-Right extremists or other zealots can be enlightening as to why so many people bypass their principles and support Trump. In a recent TV interview I heard Laurie from Ohio, with a tone of mild disgust, say, "Listen, I can't stand the guy, he's horrific in many ways especially to women, but he gets things done. All the other politicians on both sides are so damned principled they never get anything done. I mean I'm ok sacrificing some principles now and then if we can finally get some damn results." Chris from Indiana railed, "I didn't vote for a Boy Scout leader, I voted for the president of my country, the leader of the free world. He's tough by God, and I'm glad of it." And there's Michael who sees me for couples and individual therapy trying to be a better husband and save his marriage, and who works for the Trump organization (not campaign) and is a big supporter: "Yeah he's a hard boss for sure, pretty crazy actually, but I didn't go to college and he hired me; I've worked hard and he's rewarded me with promotions and a high salary. He's very pro-business, which this country needs." Also recently, at a funeral for an old friend, I reunited with my two best high school friends both of whom voted for Trump. They're both smart and successful, hard-working business owners. They love arguing with me, their token liberal. "Yeah," Kenny ranted, "Trump's a piece of sh*t but at least he gets what's really going on. I mean I'm tired of a bunch of f***ing Harvard nerds and other do-gooders telling me how to run my life and my business... I work my ass off 12 hours a day, 6-7 days a week, and all I get is more regulations and more taxes which pay for people who are lazy and do no work. I'm sick of it. And God forbid I try to fire a lousy or dishonest employee who happens to be Black or female, it's guaranteed I get sued for gender or racial discrimination. It's just not right."

These Trump voters are not crazy, selfish, or stupid. They're honest, dedicated to their families, communities, and country, and are supporting Trump because they believe it's best for them and society. And yes, they acknowledge they are sacrificing their principles to feel powerful and secure and to have powerful people lead us. If we're unable to empathize with these people and their anxieties because they voted for Trump, we will not be ready to do therapy with Trump supporters or opponents.

Therapists' Response to Trump

> Self-estrangement, Freud shows, protects us from a threatening affinity with all we have tried to disown.... Nothing that is human is alien, but nothing that is human can do without the idea of the alien, to protect itself.
>
> —Adam Phillips (p. 16)

The dialogue amongst us liberals, including us psychotherapists, seems mostly to ignore the inescapability of these human instincts. Our dialogue projects Trump and his crew as an aberration and maintains that there must be something wrong with these crazy, inhumane people who would commit these unjust, cruel, and corrupt behaviors. For the first year of his presidency we seemed obsessed with diagnosing Trump as mentally ill (how ironic for many therapists, given their general disdain for diagnosis and the medical model because it has been overly pathologizing). Trying to diagnose him away made us feel better but was ineffectual, as his people (rightfully) scoff at this pathetic use of psychological knowledge to demonize. We now seem, thankfully, to have moved away from that folly, but our dialogue continues painting Trump and clan as the alien "other," which not only emboldens and energizes them, but fuels the political polarization in the country. And our alienating attitude towards Trumpians leaves us psychotherapists uncentered, ungrounded and unable to be our most effective therapist selves

Uses, Misuses, and Abuses of Power **67**

when dealing with this topic in our sessions.

In particular we should recognize that to truly understand and relate to another human being whom we don't like, we don't pathologize or objectify them; instead we look inside ourselves for the ways we can identify with that person, and in Trump's case this means gaining a greater self-awareness of our own selfish and power-oriented urges and behaviors. This self-knowledge and empathy leave us more grounded and objective and better able to listen un-judgingly to our clients. Isn't that what we try to model and teach to clients when they come in upset or scared by their spouse, their boss, or their parents? If we support our clients' objectification of their spouses, bosses, and parents, it's a disservice to them and their relationships. Why would this be different when dealing with their reactions to Trump and his supporters? As therapists one of our talents and teachings is to distinguish between the person and their behaviors. We want to love and value the whole person, even while we judge, despise and oppose their awful, hurtful, and dysfunctional actions. I haven't seen us making that distinction with Trump and his supporters, which leads me to worry that we will model these dehumanizing "othering" biases with our clients, or support the clients' pre-existing use of othering. I understand that othering can be a successful strategy for politicians, fundraisers, and demonstrators trying to rally their troops, but I believe it is contraindicated in good psychotherapy.

How Did this Happen?

For sure, we've been thrown off by the Trump phenomenon. We weren't prepared for his victory and its consequences. We assumed Clinton would win, so we hubristically overlooked her huge flaws as a candidate. Collectively our cohort of smart successful progressives, spoiled by unprecedented advances of human rights, humanistic ideals and democratic principles since the 1960s, took it for granted that our progressive principles would prevail and continue to grow. Like the mythical Narcissus, we were looking at our own reflection (not outside of us) and fell in love with our own image.

Our sudden loss of power and status in these times of Trump is a collective narcissistic injury. This is evidenced by our entitlement, magical thinking, fear, and impotent rage—all classic characteristics of narcissistic wounding. Narcissistically we act entitled to our humanistic ideals—that they are automatic—rather than realizing that justice is an ongoing battle that we have to fight and sacrifice for in perpetuity. Narcissistically, we magically thought that conservative, Machiavellian ideologies were an endangered species on their way out, no longer to be concerned about, despite thousands of years of human history to the contrary. And narcissistically we rage and whine impotently that we are now being mistreated and ignored, rather than finding effective powerful ways to channel our anger and combat this plague.

We were scared and felt helpless, and frightened people objectify the perceived threatening of others.

The Reality of Survival Instincts

No one is immune or has evolved out of their survival instincts; all of our decisions and actions are influenced to some extent by our survival instinct and its drive to attain or retain power. There are many extinct tribes no longer on this earth and there's a good argument they are gone because they were not brutal, paranoid, or ruthless enough. To start understanding and stop denying this brutal reality, we will need to start recognizing our own tendencies toward autocratic behaviors and stop projecting these unwanted self-parts onto Trump and his followers and then othering them. An increased self-awareness of our own (unwanted) power motives will make us better informed therapists, less likely to fall into panicked thinking and overidentification with our clients. We will better hold the therapeutic space for clients, providing a stronger, safer container where their feelings are understood and not rejected or overidentified with.

Self-Awareness

> Yesterday I was clever, so I wanted to change the world. Today I am wise, so I am changing myself.
>
> —Rumi

Clinical wisdom often starts with self-awareness; this is especially true for relational and experiential therapists (as in AAP) who utilize the self in their psychotherapy. In trying to do therapy during the Trumpocracy, it's critical for us to look deeply into our selves to understand human power instincts and wishes.

Let's look in the mirror and, unlike Narcissus, look past our false, idealized self-image. Let's look instead at our full and authentic selves, our flawed human selves, the dark parts—bullying, rage, racism, greed, sexism, etc.—along with our more enlightened parts. Doing so helps us organically understand the dynamics underlying the current political situation including Trump's crude behavior, Laurie, Chris, Michael, and Kenny's votes for Trump, and everyone's fascination with this destructive evil. Owning our split-off self-parts will help us stop projecting them onto these "buckets of deplorables" and then excoriating them accordingly. From a place of heightened self-awareness grows compassion and empathy, and the prospect of viewing them as our fellow citizens, our nation's brothers and sisters who bleed just like us, get scared just like us, and over-react with bravado, just like us.

> Everyone lies, cheats, pretends (yes you too and, most certainly, I myself).
>
> —Shelly Kopp (p. 165)

Psychotherapists, and I myself, are no exception to Kopp's maxim. We all act differently when we are in power (as parents, teachers, therapists, governing officials, conference chairs, etc.) than when we are in positions of need or vulnerability. We are susceptible to lying, cheating, and deceiving, sometimes in the service of good leadership, sometimes to its detriment. When in positions of power, I have committed or witnessed lying, cover-ups, false news (or propaganda), gaslighting, exclusion, etc. Was I empowered or inebriated? Courageous or corrupted? I hope these were all done for the greater good of the organization and the profession, but I'm sure they wouldn't all ultimately be judged that way. Power changed me, I saw the world differently and justified actions very differently.

Owning our own power misuse helps us be more centered when treating our clients who are dealing with power misuse in their lives. Accepting our own Trump-like impulses frees us from shame, facilitating highly nuanced perception of a client's tone, language usage, facial expressions, body posture, and transference when they are complaining about the Trumpocracy. Likewise with politically conservative clients, rather than internal reactivity and judgment, increased self-awareness of my selfish power drives and corrupted behaviors allows me to better sit with them non-judgmentally and lovingly, even while disliking or loathing their politics. Denying or dissociating from our brutal survival impulses and power drives dampens our clinical perceptiveness and creates shame-based blind spots.

Some Conclusions

Whether looking at U.S. history or that of almost any large organization, it seems reasonable to conclude that misuses of power, large and small, are endemic and occur regularly, and probably this is a surprise to no one. Just in my short lifetime, my country has undergone a steady stream of corruption and leadership crises prior to Trump's current attempts to destroy or circumvent democracy: McCarthyism, Viet Nam, assassination plots, Nixon and Watergate, Clinton's lies and cover-up re Monica Lewinsky, Iraq's supposed weapons of mass destruction, and the corruption and financial collapse of 2008, to name only a few. It seems like the end of one leadership crisis becomes the beginning of another...and the cycle continues.

It appears that human nature, in combination with large-group dynamics, ensures that—even in progressive democratic systems—there will periodically and predictably be misuses of power, suspension of moral/ethical values, and challenges to existing rule structures. The reality of human nature and the nature of power dynamics conclusively indicate this cycle is with us to stay. If misuse of power is endemic to life, it is incumbent upon therapists to address this issue with their clients as part of any comprehensive therapy. Consequently, therapists need to address power issues within themselves and learn about their own shame and rage triggers so they don't act them out in the countertransference.

When we therapists are better able to acknowledge and understand our own power dynamics of corruption and complacency, we will better help our clients and others deal with today's Trumpocracy. Not processing these issues paradoxically risks us replicating much of Trump's dynamics, i.e., projecting our dark side onto those "crazy, White trash, racist" others and treating them with contempt, prejudice and shaming, or (unconsciously) bonding with our clients around our mutual contempt, prejudice, and shaming. This doesn't help our clients.

Looking Ahead

Please don't get me wrong, I absolutely believe we humanists should be publicly criticizing and condemning Trump's degradation of human beings, democracy, and the environment, and doing everything we can to stop him. I do believe that he is dangerous, not only by causing emotional wounding and trauma, but by actually endangering the lives of millions or billions. Clinically I believe it is important for us to affirm clients' experiences of anxiety and trauma from actions by our government. But this clinical work is most effective coming from a place of understanding the suffering, fear, and striving for power of our brothers and sisters who voted for him, not from a reactionary place of projection and denial. Laurie from Ohio, Chris from Indiana, my client Michael, and my old friend Kenny are not deplorable. They are human beings who grew sick and tired of the constant gridlock and partisan bickering in government over the past 40 years while their culture and the world changed at breathtaking speed, resulting in new existential threats and the felt loss of their safety and legacy. You and I may think global warming, racism, or misogyny are bigger threats to society than immigration, business regulations, or gun control, but that doesn't justify us othering those who disagree, and it certainly doesn't help us be unbiased and centered while conducting therapy.

Legions of therapists are being called to help our clients, Democrats and Republicans, with their current experiences of power as used, misused, and abused by Trump and his supporters. For us to best answer the call we need to return to our fundamentals: awareness of our own biases and projections and staying centered and grounded in our work. ▼

References

Kopp, S. (1974). *If you meet the Buddha on the road, kill him! The pilgrimage of psychotherapy patients.* London: Lowe & Brydon Ltd.

Phillips, A. (1995). *Terrors and experts.* Cambridge, MA: Harvard University Press.

Rumi, J. (circa 1240). Retrieved from https://www.goodreads.com/quotes/551027.

If it is a despot you would dethrone, see first that his throne erected within you is destroyed.

—Khalil Gibran (1883–1931)

Polly Hart, LCSW, BCD

ATLANTA, GEORGIA
pollyphart@gmail.com

Considering Our National Mess:
Finding a Way to Talk About Politics

NATIONAL POLITICS—I WOULD SAY OUR NATIONAL MESS—FORMERLY A TOPIC SELDOM BROACHED IN THERAPY, NOW ENTERS OUR THERAPY OFFICES REGULARLY. We learned to talk about sex, then about race, then about gender, then a bit about religion, and other such touchy matters. Do we now develop a language for talking about politics? Politics have just as much impact, even more it can be argued, on the quality of our lives than many other areas of decision-making. Do we? Don't we?

The only patient who got up and left a session with me in the last 10 years was a woman, loyal to her husband of many years whose Fox News watching she despised. But she wanted no part of my mentioning "news news" vs. "entertainment news." She intellectually rejected Fox News, but found feelings of being disloyal to her spouse unbearable. Independent thinking was not for her, and she thought she knew where I was headed. She read that one right!

We can usually finesse a conversation with those who are interested in what we think, and we can never know whether an idea offered here and there could make a difference. I've continued to respectfully share political tidbits with no problems on subjects of specific interest to those I see. Values shift, like other thoughts and feelings, and by a hundred different routes. So I never know when what I say will make a difference.

Multiple source problems can be overwhelming, and the state of our national political environment seems to fit that bill, as they say. But as psychotherapists, we know strategies for dealing with an overwhelmingly complex problem: break it into parts, study up, assess what you have, consult with others, choose a part that may be workable, make a plan, then get busy.

Grappling with our national mess, I thought I knew a lot—I did not. The following is what helped me first to understand, then to decide what I wanted to do and how I wanted to talk about politics.

My wake-up call was a recent article in *The Atlantic* describing changes in our country, Matt Stewart's "The New Aristocracy" (June 2018). I was caught by surprise and appalled by this shocking, un-acknowledged, data-based look at why so many are struggling today—their anger growing ripe for harvest, as the new "privileged" class, the top 9.9%, use self-interest and influence to create an unintended consequence, an increasingly unequal and unfair society for the other 90.1%. Then I learned that I, my colleagues, and many therapists are members of this new privileged class. We do not see ourselves accurately (privilege measured not just by money, but by influence, opportunity, access to education and resources, etc.), nor have we understood our part in the mess. The demographic changes did not create our president, but the struggles of average citizens made his promises irresistible.

Other resources that I found helpful included these:

- *On Tyranny: Twenty Lessons from the Twentieth Century* by Timothy Snyder (2017). He follows each historical lesson with a directive: what to know, then what to do. Included is an account of how ordinary folks can and do act against their moral feelings, torturing others, or watching the torture of strangers who did nothing wrong except to be the "Other."
- *I Love You, But I Hate Your Politics* by Jeanne Safer, PhD (2018 podcast). A prominent psychotherapist known for her strongly held ideas in progressive politics, married to a prominent staunch Republican for 37 years, Safer discusses strategies and language that have enabled them to be devotedly together for the duration. A key point: even strongly held truths are not necessary to share. The words you use matter, so does getting your priorities in order and learning when silence is golden— sometimes a wise path when talking with those different from yourself.
- *Corruption in America* by Zephyr Teachout (2104) provides the what, why, and how of political corruption in our country—enlightening, a must for perspective, including how today's transgressions are different from the last 200 years, and more dangerous.
- *Gaslighting America* by Amanda Carter (2018). A conservative commentator explains the techniques of moving a population into unquestioning dependency on and loyalty to a single autocratic leader, exploiting human vulnerabilities beyond many in the population's ability to understand what is happening.
- *How Democracies Die* by Levitsky & Ziblatt (2018). Yes, it can happen, despite our treasured past.
- This viral video illustrating the definition of privilege in the New Aristocracy, the 9.9%: https://www.facebook.com/viralmotion/videos/1478269608969148/ The video demonstrates how growing up in an intact two-parent home, access to private education and other resources, and basic financial security give some people great advantage over others: no guaranteed outcomes, but increased opportunity, a different starting line.

These resources helped me break down the overwhelm, make sense of the mess, and find a way to talk about and take action in response to the current political environment— though if my patients are not ready to hear, these insights don't have to be shared. ▼

References:

If someone doesn't understand privilege, show them this:

(2017). Viral Motion Facebook. Retrieved at https://www.facebook.com/viralmotion/videos/1478269608969148/

Carter, A. (2018). *Gaslighting America: Why we love it when Trump lies to us.* New York: HarperCollins.

Levitsky, S. & Ziblatt, D. (2018). *How democracies die.* New York: Penguin Random House, Crown Publishing.

Safer, J. (Speaker). (2018) *I love you, but I hate your politics: How to protect your intimate relationships in a poisonous partisan world.* New York: Macmillan Podcasts.

Snyder, T. (2017). *On tyranny: Twenty lessons from the twentieth century.* New York: Tim Duggan Books.

Teachout, Z. (2014). *Corruption in America: From Benjamin Franklin's snuff box to Citizens United.* Cambridge, MA: Harvard University Press.

Fences. 2007 by Susan Sermoneta

Beulah Amsterdam

Annihilation Anxiety

I AM SCARED. Our country is being traumatized by detention camps, children kept in cages, nuclear war looming, vicious attacks on the press, racism, loss of health care, and the rising tide of hate. Democracy seems endangered. Some of us have annihilation anxiety that includes fears of imminent catastrophe and endangerment expressed in diverse symptoms—nightmares, numbness, depression, over-reactivity, rage, avoidance, denial, vigilance, and compartmentalization. Earlier traumas get triggered anew. Past and present fears conflate.

I grew up with a fear of death like many of the refugees who seek asylum at our southern border. As a first-generation American child of Jewish immigrants, I was born when the Nazis were opening the concentration camps for the Holocaust. By age 7 I knew that the Nazis had murdered my family in Poland. Learning about the annihilation of 6 million European Jews, including my grandparents, aunts, uncles, and cousins, made me fear that I too might be murdered.

In addition to this intergenerational trauma, my own personal experience of early abandonment and severe physical and emotional abuse compelled me to deal with trauma repeatedly over the past 80 years. Psychotherapy has enabled me to become more conscious of my life-long experience with annihilation anxiety and how it is reactivated by the current political environment.

During the 2016 Republican debates, Trump displayed charisma, oratorical power, theatricality, and an endorsement of White supremacy that evoked Hitler. As Trump triumphed, I managed my dread by being as proactive as possible. Prior to their nominating convention, I emailed every Republican senator a letter that included the following:

BEULAH AMSTERDAM, PhD, pursued a path of healing from an early age, after trauma that began at her birth. Her journey has included psychotherapy, meditation, painting, and writing. Because of health issues, she retired from practice at age 60 and turned her attention to writing. She is grateful to her therapists, teachers, and writers group. Her deepest thanks goes to her husband, Ezra, for his loving and literary support for the past 53 years. *beulahamsterdam@gmail.com*

Nobody believed that Hitler could succeed in the democratic, highly cultured, scientifically advanced and educated German nation. Hitler was appointed chancellor in January 1933. In February the Reichstag was burned down, and in March Hitler opened Dachau, the first German concentration camp. Will Trump open concentration camps for Mexicans and Muslims?

I asked the senators to advocate for a convention rule change that would release delegates to vote their consciences on the first ballot.

Three months into Trump's presidency, I felt relieved that nothing like Hitler's Reichstag fire had happened and no concentration camps had been opened. But we now know that Trump's team was then planning camps for refugees.

Trump's presidency is challenging my faith that American democracy will survive. After the end of World War II, I felt great hope and joy in the founding of the United Nations. Democracy became my refuge, shield, and protection from genocide and annihilation and gave me the hope that I'd be treated decently and fairly when I became a free adult citizen. But the democracy shield is crumbling. Faith and trust have disappeared into cages. Once again I feel the fear and grief that permeated my childhood.

I am telling my story to share how I coped, survived, and thrived despite the kind of severe physical and emotional abuse that typically results in victims spending their lives in prison or mental institutions. I hope that traumatized refugees will be given therapeutic help as I was as a child.

My father's suicide just after my 1937 birth left my mother in mourning during the first two years of my life. Corpse-like, she lay in her bed near my crib, sometimes crying. Aunt Rosie, my mother's cousin, took care of me during the day. At night, during endless hours of darkness, I cried for Aunt Rosie until I fell asleep. Aunt Rosie moved away when I was turning 2. I begged, raged, cried, and screamed to go see her, a block away, but we rarely did.

Finally, Mama woke up from the dead during my third year of life. She took me outside to play in front of the red brick building where we lived on Daly Avenue down the street from the Bronx Zoo.

My first direct experience of killing and death was when I was 3. At the butcher shop, a muscular man cut off a red chicken's head. The chicken ran around the counter spurting blood until it died. When I cried, "Help the chicken," Mama and the butcher laughed. Weeks later, my brother was guarding Mama's freshly baked lemon cookies. When I touched one, he hurled me into the wall. Knocked unconscious, I lay on the floor with a big bump on my forehead. When I regained consciousness, Mama walked toward me with a big knife like the butcher's. I screamed, terrified that she was about to cut off my head. Instead, she put the cold blade on my forehead to reduce the swelling.

The recent photos of young migrant children in cages bring back the trauma of being tied down in a Fordham Hospital bed for 6 weeks when I had pneumonia at age 4. When I was rolled out of the emergency room and put in a room by myself, I screamed for Mama until I fell asleep that night. The next day, I was taken to the children's ward on the condition that I would not scream or cry. Through the glass cubicles (cages), I saw dead children on stretchers, their heads covered by white sheets, being rolled out of the huge hospital ward. I feared that I'd be taken out like them and buried deep in the ground where I couldn't breathe, and Mama would never find me.

While other children cried loudly, I wept quietly, especially when parents came with hugs, kisses, and goodies. Stories rolled through my mind—Chicken Little crying that the sky was falling, Little Red Riding Hood and the wolf, the fairy godmother in "Cinderella" getting me ready to go to the ball. Hour after hour, I untied the knots in the cords that bound my wrists and ankles to the bed.

Five weeks after I was admitted, Mama visited me for the first time. She had not brought my clothes, so she couldn't take me home with her. Another week, another eternity, went by till she came and got me. Deeply hurt and angry, I did not talk to her as she pushed my stroller homeward across the Bronx.

Pearl Harbor was bombed weeks later. When my mother's elderly Aunt Annie came for a rare visit, they wept and whispered in the kitchen. I was banished to the living room where I played with my six dolls. My 7-year-old brother was also banished when he got home from school. As we listened to the weeping in the kitchen, my brother decapitated my doll. I called out to my mother, but she said not to bother her. When I ran into the kitchen to tell her, Mama raised her hand and told me to shut up. All my dolls were destroyed. I never had a doll again.

Concentration camps were liberated the year I was 7. I learned about the German death camps from photos and articles in the *New York Times*. Grimm's fairy tales blended into fantasies and nightmares of trying to escape fiery ovens, gas chambers, mass graves, and death marches.

My mother repeatedly warned me that my older brother would kill me and insisted that I always stay in the kitchen under her protection. When he found me in another room, he suffocated or strangled me until I screamed and my mother came in. Mad that I left the kitchen, she beat me brutally. We never discussed the Holocaust; we enacted it. My brother blamed me for the disappearance of our father when I was born, and he never forgave me. Father's suicide was the family secret.

As a result of these terrifying experiences with abandonment and abuse, I became very shy, introverted, and avoidant. While at home, I raged and screamed at Mama because she refused to tell me about my father, never remembered my birthday, but always celebrated my brother's and always favored him. Severely beaten, I withdrew into weeks of silence. School was my refuge. I functioned above grade level by compartmentalizing, repressing, and denying my home experiences.

My life-long journey of emotional healing began at the public library in sixth grade when I read Freud's case studies. I was relieved to learn about other people who struggled with and overcame terror.

Days later my mother slashed my face with the buckle end of a belt, narrowly missing my eyes. I wrote to the New York City Department of Welfare asking to be sent to a Home. Six months later, a social worker appeared at our house and referred us to Jewish Family Services for counseling. Thus began my long career as a client and, later on, a psychotherapist.

At 14, I felt competent in my job at the Five and Ten, and I was angry that Mama did not let me do anything in her kitchen, not even wash dishes. She'd say that I was just a baby and didn't know how to do anything except study. Her repeated humiliation enraged me. When I picked up a knife to slice a piece of rye bread for myself, Mama glared. Her face turned red. She said, "You don't know how to cut." I continued slicing. She tried to wrestle the knife away from me. I held onto it. She raised her hand to smack me. I pointed the knife at her. She turned and ran. I threw the knife at her. I missed.

Annihilation Anxiety

After that terrifying encounter, I had recurring nightmares in which I murdered my mother while she slept in the bed next to mine. When I woke up, I was numb until I heard her snore or breathe, and I felt reprieved. Guilt consumed me and I feared that I'd spend my life in prison or a mental institution as my mother repeatedly predicted.

I consider myself very lucky and grateful to Jewish Family Services that I escaped the fate of many abandoned and severely abused children. Besides periods of individual therapy, I participated in a therapy group for teenagers, where I connected with peers who also struggled with over-controlling, humiliating parents. I revealed my rage, and they still accepted me and became my friends.

While attending the City College of New York, I lived for two years at the Girls Club of Brooklyn, a therapeutic residence originally founded to help Holocaust survivors. My refugee friends had been hidden away in closets, in convents, and under barns where they lost their identities. Some were barely functional and were in and out of mental hospitals. The Girls Club provided me with a room of my own, three tasty meals a day, community, dance and art therapy, and three sessions a week of psychotherapy.

These experiences led to my becoming a clinical psychologist and eventually an associate clinical professor at the University of California, Davis (UCD) in the department of psychiatry, where I lectured, did research studies, and supervised graduate students and psychiatry residents for over 20 years. While teaching I published "Coping with Abuse: Adolescents' Views" in Victimology. I met with young men at a juvenile prison to learn about their histories. Their experiences with family violence were similar to mine.

Trauma tends to be passed on from generation to generation, and in order to minimize anxiety in the future, individuals and families need trauma-based healing and psychotherapy. As a young mother, I became afraid of my reactivity and rage, so I sought further therapy. Since 1972, I have worked with several individual and couples therapists. I also meditated, wrote poetry, plays, stories, and memoir, and painted, giving expression to my dark feelings.

Since my issues were pre-verbal, I sought somatic therapy in the 1970s. I sat on my therapist's lap and snuggled as I never was allowed to do with Mama. Kicking a mattress, I screamed, "I hate you, Mama." During those 8 years, I came to accept my full range of feeling. I also participated in and later led somatic exercise groups designed to develop a sense of embodiment and greater awareness of oneself.

I began my private practice in 1980 in order to do individual somatic psychotherapy. But I felt unsafe and anxious while clients released their rage, so I returned to psychodynamic talk therapy.

Throughout my many years of therapy, I'd never explored my annihilation anxiety. I returned to therapy 12 years ago, and I am very grateful for my therapist's understanding and insights about how my early trauma and continuing anxiety affect my relationships.

Despite Trump's election, I still felt relatively happy and safe living in Davis, CA, where we'd thrived for almost 50 years. But in July, 2017, when a local imam called for the annihilation of all Jews, everywhere, I was triggered. Psychotherapist colleagues cautioned me to stop publishing my letters in the local newspaper condemning the imam's genocidal words. Preoccupied and obsessed with the imam's call for my "annihilation," I shared my fear of being a target in the rising tide of antisemitism. My therapist supported my continuing to publish letters on this issue. As the year went on, she repeatedly pointed out the pattern and layers of annihilation experiences starting at my birth and continuing into my adult life when I faced physicians' (mistaken) terminal diagnoses and the losses associated with aging. Without my psychotherapist, I would not have had the insight to integrate my annihilation experiences, nor the perspective to write this essay.

Recent immigration policies have further triggered my annihilation anxiety. Refugees look to America for the right to be treated equally and fairly, but upon arriving at the southern border they encounter the same terror they fled. The caged children at the border have endured terrible abuses. Not only are they experiencing isolation and abandonment, but during their imprisonment some have been severely mistreated by guards who have sexually and physically assaulted them. Their spirits have been destroyed, and many of them will become numb. When they are reunited with their families, some children refuse to talk with their parents because they have lost all sense of trust and connection.

I hope that they will receive therapy at family service agencies like I did. Family therapy could provide them with the tools to cope with trauma. Yoga can help these children to overcome numbness by bringing them back to feeling at home and comfortable in their bodies. Meditation classes in schools and community centers can teach children how to use breath as an anchor to calm and ground themselves. Above all, these children and families should be encouraged to openly discuss their traumatic experiences rather than repress them.

But I fear that these children will not have the resources available to them that I did. We must advocate for these traumatized families and children to receive the help they need to deal with their anxiety, depression, and fears of being abandoned and caged. Although children are resilient, psychotherapy will be critical in helping them heal and move forward. I hope that they will have the opportunity to live fulfilling lives, despite the trauma.

Like millions of Americans, I struggle with helplessness, terror, and rage as I hear the news. As a child I was alone. Now I have family, friends, and therapists with whom to share the pain and to confront Trump's destructive actions and the rising tide of hate and crimes against all minorities, including Jews like me. We must collectively sustain reality and sanity during this corrupt, chaotic, and catastrophic presidency. Despite anxiety, depression, and rage, we must not become numb or shrink away from our national crisis. ▼

I'm a Loser: a tanka tale*

By Neal Whitman

sushi bar patrons
watch sumo wrestling
TV on mute –
I order blowfish stew
and wake up dead

October 25, 1986: my "little boy" upper lip quivers and my two hands cover my face to hide my sobs from my wife. The ball had rolled between the legs of Bill Buckner. WTF ... I was a 38-year old-man crying over a team playing in a city where I had not lived since the third-grade. Yet, my whole life I had remained emotionally committed to the Boston Red Sox. Remember when Timmy told Lassie, "Get help!"? I got help and *got over it.*

November 8, 2016: my wife and I are in shock. "Our" network, MSNBC, called the Election and we shut off the TV. It was not yet a plan, but the next day I could not bear to turn on the set and listen to the same folks who had assured us for a year that there would be nothing to worry about, now explain what went wrong. That "Day After" I felt regret as I counted up the many hours per day that I had turned on the TV to listen to pre-event analysis, watch an event, and then listen to post-event analysis.

it's the opposite
of eating potato chips –
once I stopped watching
TV cable news shows
I could not tune in again

Lesson finally learned: losing feels worse than winning feels good.

p.s. That big box in our family room is now a "Movie-Watching" machine.

---

*Inspired by Japanese poetry, a "tanka tale" combines tanka poems with short prose.

Lisa Kays

Can Politics Be Pathology?

WAS THE CHILDREN BEING TAKEN FROM THEIR PARENTS AND CAGED THAT DID IT. That brought the outside world into sessions in a way that it hadn't before. Something about the children permeated the therapy walls more than election day, "Lock her up," journalists being threatened, Russian interference, blatant racist, misogynist, and ableist remarks at the highest levels of leadership, or the Muslim travel ban.

My colleagues have been surprised to hear that few of my patients brought the election into the therapy room, even in the weeks that followed. One or two patients were profoundly disturbed, but it otherwise went unmentioned. I seemed to be the most rattled person in my practice with no one mentioning it at all in the group I run with a colleague at 8:30 on Wednesday mornings. Meanwhile, colleagues described talking about nothing else that Wednesday.

I can admit, with shame, that I let being rattled seep out. I projected that my gay patients might feel more personally threatened than others, so I sent them emails "checking in" after the election and prior to our session. I also wrote to those working in politics at various levels. "Are you okay?" I asked.

This was odd clinical behavior for me; I was aware of that. In reflecting on "doing it" or "not doing it," I remember thinking that this was a unique situation, that it was important to show solidarity with those who might feel threatened or alone.

As a result, my patients—at least those I reached out to—were nonplussed. Or, "fine."

I now speculate that demonstrating my unsettledness to them, not exactly a hallmark of fine parenting or

LISA KAYS is a White, straight, cis clinical social worker in private practice in Washington DC, where she works with individuals, couples, and groups. In addition to traditional psychotherapy, her professional adventures include the integration of improv with therapy, and her Improv for Therapists classes have been featured on *NBC4* and in *The Washington Post*. She has also recently delved into teaching diversity at the MSW level and is increasingly interested in working with themes of race, diversity, privilege, and oppression. She lives in Washington, DC, with her husband and young son, all of whom are awaiting the arrival of their newest family addition this winter.
lisa@lisakays.com

Can Politics Be Pathology?   **81**

therapeutic leadership, left them feeling they needed to be fine to keep the ship steady.

It was the only time in my career, even my years as a fledgling intern, that I parentified my patients and put my needs first, though under the guise of caring for them. It was a reminder of the subtle lines that can be crossed in relationships between seeming care and concern that bafflingly feels selfish to the recipient.

So, in my practice, politics and the election went largely unnoticed. I attributed it to people needing space to focus on themselves, given that we were all bombarded constantly with bizarre and alarming news.

For me, though, it was loud and conspicuous. In therapy groups in which I am a patient, it was present, not always at my initiation. I remember the first thing said in my Wednesday group the day after the election was, "Can we talk about what just happened last night?" That group is relatively homogenous in political views, including the therapists, and there were many weeks of venting, alarm, and sharing personal sentiment, including by one of the therapists. I found this at times reassuring and helpful, but when his views differed from mine, frustrating. Oddly though, I wouldn't express my frustration.

It didn't feel safe for some reason. This was real, now. This wasn't transference and maybe you remind me of my father. This was, "I could really offend you," or "We could be truly opposed about something for which I won't be forgiven." That didn't feel like territory worth treading into. I still think about that.

It reminded me that the power I carry with patients is not benign and cannot be set aside. I see disagreements about politics as disagreements about fundamental values, family histories, economic status and worthiness, and one's place in the world. It is about judgment and acceptance, even the right to exist, to be attached, to be part of the group. As we all know, there is nothing scarier or more threatening than to be cast out.

In another group, the views were not so homogenous. I lashed out directly—and, I was told, unfairly—at those on "the other side." I still struggle to see that unfairness. Can we disconnect the political behavior of someone from its outcome? Why, with politics, must I politely step aside and say, "Well, these are just ideas," when those ideas are often directly harmful, even deadly, to others?

If I went up to an immigrant on the street and screamed, "You don't belong here!" or worse, physically assaulted them, as people did on Metro trains in DC, I would be condemned by most, I hope. But if I act on that same belief in a voting booth and give someone else the power to execute it, it is ok?

At what point do hands become dirty?

It has been two years since election day 2016 and my initial inappropriate clinical reaction. Politics has become a relative non-issue in therapy, even for me, as I worked through my reactions and tried to develop a more mature stance towards those I disagree with.

Until they separated the children from their parents.

I wasn't as reactive with my patients. I didn't launch into my terror in sessions at my own initiation. But there would be moments when it found its way in, as unconscious material does, through instinct and surprising connections. For instance, a young patient got furious at me for not fully grasping her horror at her neighborhood's gentrification. The interaction and disconnect between us felt unusual and out of character, so I gently asked, "Are you following the news at all?" She melted into tears and described her personal connection to those at risk of deportation and her horror as an adoptee at what was happening to children at the border.

There was also the woman who discussed her marriage one day in a way that seemed more heightened and disconnected than usual. She was confused by her own reaction and recent feelings in the relationship. I found myself pointing out that her husband is White and she is a woman of color. Both are immigrants in the US. "Is what's happening in the news affecting you at all?" I asked. In this case, maybe, maybe not, she said. She was certainly aware of increased stress due to the news and what was happening, particularly, to immigrants and their children. She also revealed and explored more about her isolation and loneliness in a cross-cultural marriage, feeling she had left some of her identity behind and longed for home dearly—aspects of her marital difficulty that exist (or do they?) outside of personality conflicts or interpersonal issues. The unspoken dimension of race and culture was now in the room, and our conversation became more connected and fluent. I hope I would have found a way to that without the current political climate, but the poignancy and rawness of it helped define the lines faster. We were also able to address briefly my Whiteness and her non-Whiteness and, while nothing profound emerged in that discussion, it felt important that it was in the room.

I sat with a therapy patient who is also a graduate student last week. She is American and her heritage is Korean. As she recounted receiving a grade that seemed confusing, at best, and unfair, at worst, I found myself thinking of an article about grade irregularities for women and minorities in American universities. I wondered out loud if she suspected anything like that and asked about the demographics of her program and class. "I have wondered," she admitted, in new tears. This was followed shortly by a sheepish, "Am I crazy?" It turned out she had been sitting on feelings of racial exclusion and isolation socially and academically for a long time and had been wondering, "Am I crazy?" for just as long. This conversation might have occurred without the children being put in cages. After that though, it seems more of a certainty than a maybe.

More recently, after the Kavanaugh hearings and confirmation, a group discussion included one White woman's struggle with being in a leadership position in an organization where she was watching other leaders marginalize and treat minorities differently and, at times, unfairly. As the group discussed her situation, she explored her family's role as a bystander in the KKK-ridden South during her childhood, where she was taught "bad people did bad things to Black people" but wasn't taught that it was any of her business. "Do I do something?" she asked. "I want to, but I don't know what to do. I don't know how," she said. "Of course not," I offered. "Your experience, many of our experiences as White people, prepared you to stand by and look the other way, not to act. How could you know?" I wondered, was that an overreach? Politics and racism were not usually part of groups. Was I objective enough? Was it my role, as a social worker, not to be?

Suddenly, so much feels uncharted.

In that same group, another woman struggled with her boyfriend's not understanding her anger and fear at the Kavanaugh hearing. In fact, wasn't sure he shouldn't be confirmed. She expected the group to tell her to dump him immediately—and part of her wanted to—but no one did, and part of her didn't want to. There was much sitting in silence that day. One member said. "We can't go on with no one relating to anyone else because they don't agree." At the same time, that same person acknowledged that

Can Politics Be Pathology?

she couldn't do it, if it were her. The patient could understand the boyfriend's stance, could tie it to his past and to his experience. "Becoming woke is a process," someone acknowledged. "It takes time."

Suddenly, things feel simple and complicated at the same time.

I also see a patient who is on the opposite political side from me. He is not just a Republican; he proudly identifies with the Alt-Right. He is also not White. Our relationship began not long after the election, when he was having difficulty interacting with others and was destroying personal relationships without meaning to. I like him, and I believe that we have formed a genuine attachment. I believe it may be the most genuine attachment he has in his life. Yet, much of our relationship is unspoken, at least by me. I admit that once the children were taken from their parents, I found it harder not to say, "WHAT ON EARTH ARE YOU DOING?" Additionally, he desperately needs to be in group therapy. Were he anyone else, I likely would have put him in a group long before now. And while there are complications, such as his work and travel schedule, I am also aware of my ambivalence to place him in a group in my largely politically homogenous practice. As I said to a colleague, "He desperately needs a group. But he won't have any-one to connect to politically and may, in fact, be vilified. I'm terrified for him, for my other patients, and the group."

And I'm terrified for me. I project onto my patients my own disdain and rejection of those who tolerate intolerance. Will my patients lose respect for me for working with him? Will they feel betrayed? How will I defend and stand up for him, which would certainly be called for, without aligning with his views and principles? Certainly, I do this in our individual work, but it feels so much more threatening and vulnerable to make my "secret" known, that I am attached to someone in the Alt-Right and attempting to help him. Would they ever forgive me? Do I forgive myself? Would I forgive myself if I abandoned him or refused to help at all?

All I see before putting other patients in groups is how it would benefit them, and I know if I strip away the politics, that he is no exception. I am also aware that it is hard to imagine the benefits of attachment, honest relating, and feedback working amidst such a personal, divisive dynamic.

Can groups remain tolerant when faced with intolerance? Can we separate people from their beliefs? Can we love despite hate? On an intellectual level, I believe we can. On a visceral level, though, when it comes to real-time relationships and decisions, I find I am not so sure. Attachments are primitive. So is survival.

Children being taken from their parents is, as we know as therapists, torturous, abusive, malevolent and evil. Face to face with someone, can we discuss it, rationally and with love between us? Should we?

I don't know anymore.

It is perhaps not surprising then, my gaffs aside, that politics stayed mostly out of the therapy room until the children were put in cages.   ▼

Gina Sangster

Getting It Right

THE DECO-ERA BUILDING USED TO BE A MOVIE THEATER, AND SOME OF THE DESIGN FEATURES REMAIN, though the building owner is threatening to cover up the red-and-blue geometric lobby floor tile with a slab of something new and neutral. When I found this out, I contacted the office of historic preservation but couldn't get very far. It seems owners have a lot of freedom with the interior of structures, as long as they don't tamper with the exterior in an historic district. I grew up in an antiques-collecting family, and I like to preserve things of value.

Entering my office on the 4th floor, I switch on the white-noise machine and the two table lamps I picked up from Miss Pixie's on 14th Street, adjust the pillows on the couch, and put away my bags and lunch. I survey the room to make sure everything is in its place. I don't mind that someone else uses my space when I'm not there, but I want things to be as I like them, for my own comfort and that of my clients. Many people comment on how much they like the room: the light from the balcony sliding doors, the pictures on the wall, the small plants, the books.

These days, we are under siege, the outside world encroaching on the peaceful spaces we try to create and maintain for ourselves and our clients. Is this what it's like in Israel and Palestine? In other parts of the world where war is more the norm than the exception? Of course, our sense of disruption pales in comparison to the decades-long chaos so many people endure. We aren't lighting candles or laying down prayer rugs or hustling our children off to school in the midst of collapsing buildings, the sounds of bombs exploding nearby. But

GINA SANGSTER is a Washington, DC, native who continues to live and work in the same neighborhood where she grew up. With an MFA in poetry from Columbia University awarded in 1975, she completed the MSW at Catholic University's School of Social Service in 1986. Gina now works with individuals and couples in a diverse group private practice, along with providing clinical supervision. She continues to write both poetry and personal essays. The long and winding path of her own clinical and creative journey informs Gina's work with artists and others who may have gotten lost along the way. *gshdc@aol.com* the firewall between us and the outside world, the world we normally keep at bay in our sessions with clients, is permeable now in a way it never has been.

Can we maintain a neutral gaze when we, like our clients, have just been scrolling through a news feed that brings one more horror, one more clip of unparalleled disruption to the world we had come to take for granted? It seems many White people sleep-walked through the Obama years. I felt as though the devastation of the assassination of the Rev. Dr. Martin Luther King—which occurred as I was graduating from high school here in DC—had finally been atoned for. We could all relax—people of all colors—couldn't we? Look at our First Family! That's who represents us to the rest of the world. That's who symbolizes our best selves. Hadn't we actually "overcome" at last, as the song says? But who are "we" now in this current environment?

Therapists treat anxiety in all its forms; we help our clients cope with and hopefully rise out of depressive episodes. We work with couples to help them learn to speak to one another with compassion and understanding; to help them argue in ways that won't be destructive. We give people hope. With all of the newer modalities of therapy that continue to populate our profession, we still come back to the healing salve of listening, the curative properties of our being there, week after week, in the same place at the same time, building the corrective emotional experience one moment at a time. To what extent is the safety of the therapeutic space being threatened, both by external events of the day and our own inner turmoil?

I am more uncomfortably aware of my Whiteness now than I have been since I was a child and my family moved into a ramshackle frame house that had been slated by the city for condemnation. The word "gentrification" wasn't in the air. I was a naïve 7-year-old, and my parents were New York bohemians. I would quickly learn that it meant something that I was White and the kids next door and across the street were Black. As an only child, all I ever wanted was to fit in, to belong to a peer group, to find my tribe. In some ways, being a therapist fulfills that quest for me, particularly being part of a diverse practice group in terms of race, culture, age and sexual orientation, a group that attracts clients who are equally diverse on all dimensions. But the ground has shifted beneath our feet. I find myself feeling grateful—and relieved—that clients of color still come to see me, still choose me despite the news of the day of one more degradation suffered, one more act of home-grown terrorism, one more crazed young White boy with a gun.

And now I'm preparing to start a group focused on early loss and its implications for attachments and relationship dynamics. Early loss is a centerpiece of my own life story—from my father's death when I was 16 to my mother's death just shy of my 40th birthday. I know from my own experience—and continue to learn from others—that putting the right mix of people in a group is essential for its viability and growth. Early loss is the easy part—a client whose father committed suicide when she was a child; another whose mother died when she was a teen; a woman who lost both of her parents within a few years of one another; a young woman who was adopted at birth and whose adoptive father then died when she was an adolescent. Now it becomes a matter of who wants to make the commitment; who feels sufficiently motivated to overcome their natural trepidation about group therapy to take the leap?

Then suddenly one day in mulling this over, I am struck by the realization that I haven't considered the political dimension at all. I've been thinking about age, cultural background, and personal history, along with other factors that might make for a rich and meaningful group dynamic. But party affiliation? What if I include someone in the Trump camp? What if the conversation veers into the political terrain, as it is likely to do? I worry that this person could be vilified, that their already fragile sense of self could once again be damaged by a harsh reaction from another group member. I understand that we want our therapy groups to represent life in the world; we want our clients to benefit from real life experience in the laboratory of the group. But how much risk of conflict is tolerable? Knowing ahead of time that this very real potential exists, what should I do—or not do—to guard against it?

I want to get it right—not so "right" that I've controlled all the rough edges out of the mix of people I hope to gather together. But this feels like a different level of danger than what I had already anticipated. The toxicity of our current political climate feels so virulent, unlike anything I have experienced in my lifetime. While parts of DC were burning during the riots, I still had Black friends who had my back. I had earned their trust and respect. I was not "one of them," the bigoted Whites who controlled everything for the privileged few. Now I'm not so sure of being seen and understood. And I'm more afraid of bringing people together in a group that might explode or break down, causing just the kind of harm we work so hard to heal.

I'll borrow my friend Courtney's office for my Saturday afternoon group. It's newly decorated and larger than mine, part of our expanded 4th-floor suite. Lacking some of the unique character of my room across the hall, it offers comfort and space, and while its tall windows don't open, they give a nice view of rooftops and sky through gauzy curtains. I can feel her presence there, friend and colleague, and take comfort in that sense of familiarity while I adjust to surroundings not of my own choosing. I know that I need to let go of some of my wish to get things right and allow myself to open to possibilities, unexpected moments of connection in the midst of conflict or pain, the gifts of compassion and understanding that can arise out of shared loss. ▼

* * *

Commentary

I WAS STOPPED BY THE DILEMMA POSED BY THIS THERAPIST. I read it several times and kept feeling totally unqualified to comment. I have not convened nor been part of an ongoing therapy group in over 25 years. The more I had nothing to say, the more I noticed edges of resentment. Why did I ever say I would do this? I could feel the thin candy shell forming over my inadequacy.

During the days I was thinking about my response:

1. I heard then saw a fight break out in the parking lot of my local grocery. A man shouted threats and pounded on cars, then threw himself on the departing vehicle. Those of us who remained after the scene compared notes on our shock and disbelief. We all wanted our civility back.
2. I found myself reviewing all the therapeutic failures and blunders I accomplished throughout my long career. Some of them looked the same, some seemed different. I grieved.
3. I had a reunion with my old posture-group friends. We determined to take up the stance of "Calling the Spirits." My intention was to find a spirit teacher who might tell me more about how to manage risk while living in times of outrage.
4. I met a very soulful stag deer with a tear in his large eye. His rack of antlers was listening beyond his ears as he searched for a way through the forest.

After that encounter, I felt like something was unlocked in me. I remembered my first experience of being a patient in a therapy group. I was a newly-married young White woman and I had undertaken individual therapy to figure out my disappointments. After a time, I joined a therapy group of other White people. I do remember feeling terribly exposed and threatened at times. Authentic encounter was highly prized. Lots of unexpected events happened in the course of our time together including marathon sessions where I had big openings and deep catharsis. I got it wrong. We got it wrong, but maybe we became more human and found mercy. Somehow, I believe, we all felt we could tolerate and contain the darker dynamics of our work together.

That confidence is missing from this piece. The ground has indeed shifted. The therapist has gotten older. The "feed" follows us everywhere. But, it is still the job of the therapist to take care of one's own rage, to determine if a co-therapist will provide needed companionship and perspective, to clarify the ground rules about extraneous conversation, and to hold fast to that ground when the power gestalt of the group begins to tilt. I wonder how much of the therapist's fear for the safety of a client from the Trump camp comes from a bias of the therapist against the client's "wrong" political viewpoint. As a liberal, feminist, white haired, White woman of Irish Catholic descent, I find myself dismayed with facing my own political shadow every morning in *The Washington Post*. The work of discernment in and out of the office is taxing, but I believe that "good fences make good neighbors," as Frost tells us. Getting it wrong can be surprising and disarming and can cause damage to one's sense of self. But I think healing and recovery need to allow the unknown to arise in the consciousness of group members and their group therapist so the shadow becomes visible and accountable.

—Judy Lazarus, MSW

See Me, Seema

XANTHIA JOHNSON LPC, LCPC, ACS, RPT-S, is a licensed psychotherapist, Supreme Embrace Guru, essayist, and compassionate anti-racism consultant. Her boutique private practice, Urban Playology LLC, is in Dupont Circle in Washington, DC. Xanthia provides transformative psychotherapy and creative arts therapy to outliers, unique families, and LGBTIQA folk.
urbanplayology@yahoo.com

Author's note: As a person of color, I take note about how White people, how Black people, how Brown people may experience my writing, the nuances of it. People who reviewed this all owned their discomfort and unanswered questions about the bank backdrop. The theme of money is very important because I've been taught by society that I will never earn or "have in the bank" what a White person will have. Nevertheless, I have to try to build more wealth and legacy. In this experience, when I least expected it, something short of a miracle happened. I finally felt seen and heard—in a bank!—as a human being by another human being who also happened to be a Brown person. That had never happened before. But it did and under a political regime where I feel even more invisible as a Black woman.

MY PARTNER AND I SET OUT TO RUN ERRANDS. Little did I know that I would get to practice being seen. En route to the grocery store, we saw a branch of the banking institution where I had been intending to close an account because three months' worth of service fees totaling $60 had accumulated on an inactive account. I had received notice that the fees would kick in, but it didn't seem like three swift months had actually passed.

The branch had just opened, and I was hoping for a short wait time. I was ready to pay the $60 fine in order to zero the account. I did not think it was fair for a trillion-dollar banking institution to be charging the account of a middle-class African-American. Intellectually, I knew I wasn't the only person being charged. But in these current political times, I felt particularly offended that I was being forced to help the bank become even richer.

There was an Indian woman in an office to our right,

helping a customer. There was another person waiting in the lobby to meet with her. To our left were the teller windows, and there was no wait. In retrospect, I think my urgency was provoked by my brewing anger about feeling oppressed by yet another system that seemed to have no palpable investment in me as a human being.

I approached a White middle-aged female teller, informing her of my intent to close the account. She initially dispensed $3.45. The balance on the account was negative $60, and I didn't understand. She didn't ask why I was closing the account. She didn't try to get me to stay with the institution. She told me to call a 1-800 number to officially close the account. She said she could not furnish a printout marking the account closed, which seemed odd to me. She again assured me that if I called the 1-800 number, verification that the account had been officially closed would be sent to the email address on file. Or, she offered, we could come back in approximately 30 minutes to meet with a specialist who had not yet arrived.

One of the ways I am unconsciously affected by these times is manifest in my need for proof of record, proof of pro-active action on my part. But we left the bank without the hard copy I so desperately wanted. On our way back from the grocery store I just had to go back to the bank. Inside, we saw the same Indian woman, alone in her office. The White teller shot me a glance and looked away. An African American teller did the same.

The Indian woman eagerly got up and introduced herself as Seema, the bank manager. She quickly ushered us into her office. I was admittedly anxious, wondering if she had noticed us before. My body language was tightly closed, and I was trying to figure out how best to convey my need for the hard copy. "How can I help you?" she asked. Sometimes I experience Asian people the same as I do White people, so I brace myself. I wonder if they see me. Do they judge me? Would my heart's desire matter to them? Sometimes without realizing it, I assume Brown people other than Black people are White to protect myself from microaggressions and internalized racism. In retrospect, this is likely why I felt so anxious.

Seema listened patiently to my appeal and then began rapidly clicking her keyboard. With a curious look at her computer screen, she told us that she might not be able to furnish the hard copy but would do her best. "I'm going to do something for you if the system allows me." As she worked, Seema engaged us in light conversation.

I shared that in graduate school I nannied two bi-cultural Indian girls. Seema seemed most moved, however, by my love of yoga, wanting to know where I teach. If Seema had inquired about my private practice, she would have gotten an earful. But my yoga practice is more personal to me. As a person of color, I learned not to share the heart of me. People should earn the privilege to hear my story.

Contrary to that notion, though, it seems this unspoken rule slightly bends when one Brown person encounters another Brown person. Seema asked if I was available to teach her sister private yoga lessons in their home. Without realizing it, my body language had softened a bit. The cloud of apprehension seemed to be fading away in the climate Seema created for us.

It is important to say that White people and Brown people from other ethnicities are not the only sources of pain for me. Sometimes the most egregious meanness comes from other Black people. Intellectually I know there's always the possibility of that kind of emotional terrorism. But it still hurts. I grew up hearing other Black and Brown people urging that we should stick together. But so many of us have sought shelter in the great divide. Sometimes it feels like it's every person for themselves. This saddens me so.

In some magical way, Seema was able to recover the monthly fees and provide my beloved hard copy. She said that she couldn't understand why the fees had been instituted in the first place. She said it wasn't fair.

Seema had only two requests for me—to alert her about my next yoga class and to please give her a strong review when the customer service survey arrived in my inbox. She ushered us back to the same teller, whose demeanor was more open than what I remembered just hours before. Seema met us on the other side of the window, closely observing the transaction. This time the teller asked more customer-friendly questions "Envelope? Any specific bills you want? Would you like me to cut your debit card?" She finally gave me the hard copy that had been unavailable to me the first time around. As we left the bank, I wondered why the teller hadn't given us the option to meet with Seema earlier.

I think Seema and I both practiced being seen that day. Two Brown people seeing each other. Me allowing her to help me. Me being invited to help her. I wanted to help, and I kept my word: I screen-shot my glowing remarks on the survey and subsequently shared them with her by phone. If I don't practice being seen and being vulnerable, how can I help clients practice being seen?

Since that day at the bank, Seema and I have practiced yoga together at my home. The yoga she was arranging for her sister was actually for her. She said that she was wary about sharing such a personal thing about herself with a stranger. I told her that I totally understood. It seems that Seema had the same questions about me that I had about her—if I was trustworthy, if I was judging her, if I was safe.

As we see more of each other, I have many trepidatious and cultural questions for Seema:

Am I your only Black friend? Was your marriage arranged? Were you raised in New York? Do you have siblings? How often do you visit India, and could I visit you there? What side of the political aisle are you on? (I ask myself, do I really want to know this? Am I ready to hear the answer? And am I ready to share my liberal views with her?)

How ironic it is that I've built a practice with emphasis on anti-racism, diversity, and inclusion! Outliers, unique families, and LGBTIQA folks, most of whom are of color. In these current times, the work is a safe place for me and my clients. No matter the charged political climate here in DC, our work together is and always will be a safe place and a safe space for me and my clients.

Thank you for seeing me, Seema. My hope is that you believe I see you too.   ▼

Editor's note: The following has been lightly edited for length and clarity. Sidney Jourard and Ernest Kramer were both AAP members.

Tape #89: Interview with Dr. Sidney Jourard by Dr. Ernest Kramer

I interviewed Sidney Jourard during the 1973 meeting of the American Psychological Association. The windows of the room we met in were closed against the hot, humid weather of the Montreal August. Sounds of traffic came in from a busy downtown made busier through the piling in of thousands of psychologists.

Although Sid and I had met and talked together on previous occasions, our interview seemed to start with a certain stiffness and formality. I think a little later on we realized that part of that was due to the tape recorder sharing a room with us and the unseen listeners who might hear this tape. And having realized it, things went on a little more loosely and naturally after that.

Earlier, though, the interview began with my asking Sid about whether he still practiced psychotherapy. I've known therapists who, having done therapy and written their books on therapy, no longer saw patients but devoted themselves to writing and frequently to teaching others. In contrast to that pattern, Sid said that yes, he did still see patients in psychotherapy, but he no longer liked to teach psychotherapy, and he talked some about why.

Jourard: I want to continue to be a psychotherapist. It's one of the areas in which I like to keep growing, and I want to continue learning and writing about it, but not teaching it in the sense of training. I don't know why I stayed away from that, maybe because I think I don't like to reflect too much on what I do with my life. Also, that ties in with some of my own theoretical views about what I'm learning about how one person helps another person get on with his life.

Kramer: I understand not teaching in the classroom sense. What about the notion of supervision, individual training of another therapist? Is that foreign to you too, now?

J: It's not something I would gladly do right now. I won't say next year or five years hence, but I have no great desire right now to sit and listen to someone's tape recordings. I have feelings even about tape recording psychotherapy sessions, although I've done it before, and I've listened to them, and I've let other people listen to them. But it encourages someone to imitate himself—like if I listen to my own tapes, I'm likely to imitate myself, I think, or if somebody watches Carl Rogers or Fritz Perls or me or somebody else doing psychotherapy, I think it encourages them to try to imitate and be like Fritz Perls or Carl Rogers or like me. The problem is to help them become whoever *they* can be.

K: Let's get on to your thing of self-disclosure, that what part of yourself you disclose depends on the setting, the audience and the mechanical apparatus that's around you.

J: I'm certainly affected by whom I'm speaking to. I'm speaking to you now, but I'm also speaking to some imaginary group of patrons of the AAP Tape Library. I feel reasonably comfortable with that, but it's not the same as you and I sitting here talking just between the two of us. I think when someone is taping his sessions, it's a split commitment. And I find whether in writing or trying to help another person, I'm most effective if I'm, like

Kierkegaard said, trying to do one thing. To try to teach something and show it at the same time, I'm probably like the Zen statement, "When you sit, sit, and when you stand, stand. Don't wobble."

K: Ok, but I like the notion that there are different kinds of audiences one speaks to. I'm aware, now, of talking for an anonymous audience, too. It strikes me that something you have written about that is often missed is what I'll call "sensible self-disclosure." I think you've been misread in suggesting that everyone should disclose everything all around. That's clearly an unfair kind of reading. What you disclose to a friend, what you disclose to a single person, and to this anonymous audience, is going to be a different series of events.

J: I think that's fair. I'm glad a lot of people read what I've written. That's what I write it for. Then at workshops and lectures, someone says, well, come on, disclose more of yourself or how do you expect I'm going to disclose myself to you? Sometimes it's neither relevant to the interests of the audience or I'm not interested in what they have to say just then, or I don't want to talk about what they're asking me to talk about because we're not acquainted, and so on. There's a difference between self-disclosure and broadcasting. Self-disclosure is dialogue. It's part of what is going on between two people. You can broadcast the truth, but that's different from what I understand by authentic talk between two people.

K: So self-disclosure isn't something a person does. Self-disclosure is a style of dialogue.

J: It's just a name for speaking your truth to another person, with some consideration to what's going on between you. Is the other person interested, for example.

K: With some hope for getting truth back.

J: Yes. I sit in situations, lots of times, where someone uses this magic word, self-disclosure. They're going to disclose themselves to me. But I have no desire to listen to them, so very kindly I'll listen for fifteen, twenty or thirty minutes, as they disclose themselves. But it's driving me up the wall with boredom or embarrassment or I'm trapped 'til finally, I have to say, "Please, I don't want to listen anymore!" Then, dialogue has begun.

K: Right. I was going to lay the Gestaltist trip on you then, Sid, and suggest that maybe after five minutes, you should tell them, "I'm bored."

J: M-hm. Well, I usually will. Half an hour is a figure of speech.

K: Ok. You mentioned Kierkegaard before. My own association with Kierkegaard's emphasis on actually living the life of action or living the life of ideas into action—I'm wondering how much the notions of self-disclosure that you've written about, certainly in many aspects of life, but mainly in terms of therapy, affect your dialogue outside of the therapy situation. Not only in what you offer, but what you expect and demand of others.

J: I don't see a big difference or a gulf between, let's say, the way I try to live my life within my personal life of family and friends, and the way I live my life in the company of students or clients, patients; I don't see that there's a place to be authentic and caring and concerned for the other person and yourself, here, but not here. There's a difference in what sorts of things are appropriate in one setting or another, but I certainly try to live my truth in and out of my consulting room, in and out of my classroom, in and out of my house, in and out of your house—

K: Isn't that risky?

J: Yes...

K: I've tried some of it. I like the notion, but it doesn't strike me as invariably rewarding.

J: Well, sometimes it's very punishing, but I find it more enlivening than, I don't know, trying to pretend to be somebody else, which I find very tedious and very boring. I've tried to cut that out of my life as much as possible.

K: Ok. For historical bent—who did you use to pretend to be?

J: Oh, I don't know, all kinds of heroes! And not only heroes but whoever my mother thought I should be and my father thought I should be, and whoever I thought I should be, and my teachers at Toronto—whoever they thought I should be—

K: How about when you started doing psychotherapy?

J: Oh, I think I started out being a mimic of Carl Rogers and a mimic of Sigmund Freud as I understood him from his writings on technique, and wherever I could find anybody to mimic, I mimicked them until it got to be awkward, absurd, ridiculous—fortunately, harmless. I was just making an ass out of myself. I don't think I hurt anybody while I was doing it. I think I started to learn how to be a psychotherapist when I paid less attention to my style and more attention to who I was with and what we were there for and how our dialogue was unfolding.

K: How come you started doing that?

J: That's a good question. I think because, at a time when I started to have to learn to earn part of my living doing psychotherapy, in Atlanta, Georgia, I was still heavily under the influence of my Buffalo training, which was a mixture of Rogerian and neo-Freudian, Sullivanian, that sort of emphasis. The people who consulted with me were primarily Southerners from Atlanta, and rural Georgia, and they weren't particularly sophisticated psychotherapy patients the way people in normal clinics, city clinics were. As I talked like a medically-oriented or -influenced psychotherapist with a great deal of impersonal technique, the patients thought I was crazy in the first place, absurd in the second, and let me know that I wasn't being very helpful.

K: If the patients let you know you weren't being helpful, you were in some kind of real dialogue. I've seen it hurt bad there and so have you.

J: M-hm.

K: I've been a patient with bad therapists, and I don't let a bad therapist know when I think he's lousy. I just cut out. Or, if I do let him know, he's never going to hear it. It must have been something you were doing, even in your masquerade days, that got through and allowed people to tell you, "Hey, what's going on?"

J: Well, I think I cheated a little bit in the sense that I went against what I took to be some of the precepts of my training. I would share whatever I as a human being had experienced about problems like the ones we were talking about just then, and how other people talked about it. What made it embarrassing was the idea that if you are a psychotherapist, you shouldn't at all be like a helpful uncle or aunt or, well, like somebody sharing an experience as they do in *Reader's Digest*, or something like that. But, that's actually a very helpful thing to do with another human being. At least I've found it so, and also, whenever I've been a patient—which hasn't been often, in a formal sense, but from time to time I do turn to my colleagues when I'm down—I'm keenly interested in how they, as human beings, wrestle with problems that I'm wrestling with.

K: So the start of the change is that, probably with some feelings of guilt, you went against your academic conscience, and behind closed doors, let somebody know who you were, and then they could tell you the foolish parts of yourself, too. They could then tell you when you haven't been real to them.

J: I think that the people who consulted with me, even when I was in training, but also when I began as a private practitioner, really, almost in Skinnerian terms, shaped me up or taught me how to be the kind of a therapist who would be effective with persons like them. And I have found no reason to revert back to the impersonal, anonymous, slick technician that at one time I thought was the proper way to be. I'll tell you who influenced me; it was people like Carl Whitaker, John Warkentin and Tom Malone, in that Atlanta group, because this is where I was first functioning as an independent, part-time, private practitioner, and they were renegades in Atlanta.

K: To some extent, literally, one of the things you learned from the Atlanta bunch was to walk in and look at your own craziness. Now, I've got my own bias. It is my value system that until you can do that, one, I don't think you can be very creative, and two, it is just too great a risk to expose yourself to the craziness of somebody else.

J: I come from a background where that is one of the first expressions you hear when you do something that goes counter to what is regarded as right and proper and respectable. I can just hear my parents or relatives saying, "Oh, you're crazy! You're crazy!" I grew up in an atmosphere where the right way to do or be was clearly defined. This is Toronto, and the whole Jewish tradition, "If you do that, you're crazy!" was part of my background. I've always been as crazy as a loon although I've concealed a lot of it. I'll never forget, one session when I was particularly full of self-loathing, as I was exploring something that neither Whitaker nor Malone were particularly interested in (they didn't encourage you talking about your real-life peccadillos, and I had a lot of peccadillos to review). Apropos of nothing, Whitaker was sucking on his pipe and said, "I'll never forget the first time I heard somebody call me a psychopath. It was at a psychiatric conference, and I was presenting this paper in perfectly good faith, and there was a hushed silence after it was over, and from the rear, I heard someone of my colleagues say, 'Why that man is a psychopath!' That was one of the most relieving things."

K: Helped you set your goal, Sid?

J: Yes, it made me feel much better about myself.

K: I don't get to be called a psychopath very often, because I haven't been that successful, but the notion that somebody who chooses his path and works at it successfully, is going to be called a psychopath, rings true to me.

J: Oh, yes! And as near as I can understand, in order to hang on to whatever I would regard as the alive and really good, essential parts of me, I've got to be resourceful, energetic, cunning, and so on, and I know that my aim in this world is not to lie, cheat, steal, murder, rape, or misrepresent myself. I also know that in order to make some kind of contribution, I have found it necessary to be all those things—energetic, alert, imaginative, creative, and at times, cunning.

K: I guess that goes back to the theme of choice of situation for self-disclosure, when cunning must come in. When I'm with a patient who has paid me or who is in an institution that pays me, and he's come for help, even if it costs me a fair bit of pain, I'm going to try to be not only honest but actively self-disclosing to him because I see it as a healing thing. But I'm not about to offer that socially, in many situations.

J: Well, I agree with that because I really do believe that the authenticity of my participation is what is helping the other person come more to life. This doesn't mean that I don't govern what I say to another human being with some tact or consideration for the other person's feelings. Although I can say blunt things. In some of my close friendships, I am a loving friend but I can say a blunt thing when I think it's helpful and appropriate. In social situations, I can play appropriate social games. I'm glad I can.

K: Do you teach your patients to do it?

J: Sure! What could be more helpful in group and individual therapy than to train people to get into the community? I think in the rehabilitation wing of every psychiatric hospital should be drama coaches so that, along with learning how to live more comfortably with their own feelings and in their own bodies, and how to be honest where it's called for, there's a place for teaching people how to act.

K: So you need two sets of capabilities. One is a capability for being authentic and self-disclosing, and the other is the capability for hiding with some cunning and protection. Then, you need to be able to choose which is appropriate.

J: Yes, I think my whole theory about personal growth and development is that it's an endless process of adding to your degrees of freedom of movement and expression. It's better to be able to do two things than one; it's better to be able to do three than two.

K: I remember that in some of your research, you're finding that some of the most self-disclosing individuals were those seen as deeply disturbed and neurotic, and it struck me that perhaps those were the ones who self-disclosed out of some inner compulsion and couldn't choose to shut it off.

J: Without any empathy or so great was their need, you might say that they couldn't receive any signals as to whether it was appropriate to spill their guts just then. And so, in a way, they were stuck in one way of being, sort of a compulsive need to be known and heard by everybody, looking for someone who would then respond helpfully.

Then, the other extreme is people who are like the public Nixon. I don't know what the private Nixon is like, but the public Nixon appears to do anything rather than let anyone know what he's really up to. In some ways, he represents a great deal of the American culture, I think. He embodies it. He could be regarded as an exemplar of a way of being that seems to have paid off for people who want to be upwardly mobile which is to get power and wealth that always seek to produce an impression and never let the truth get in the way. Impressions sell goods and impressions get votes or lose votes, and that's almost a metaphor for the way a lot of people out of big business and politics live their lives.

K: Why not just become him? What happens if you give up the self-disclosure to decide that you will be the most attractively packaged article on the market in every situation? You'll just change the wrappings.

J: Of course, a lot of my clientele have been people who have lived that way, up to the point where they became the somebody looking for help. And it was because in relating in that image-producing way, not just with their customers and clients, but also with their closest friends and family, they found themselves knowing that the other person was not addressing them.

K: M-hm.

J: Knowing that the other person did not know them, so they felt lonely and out of touch, because they grew out of touch.

K: The bind is then, if I always hide my real self, no one loves me for myself; they love me for the package that I was wrapped in.

J: Right. That metaphor is so exact. The historian will have to look at this age, let's say in America, as the advertising age, the triumph of J. Walter Thompson and John B. Watson, the triumph of image over reality until people begin to look inside the package and want to know what's in it. But it sure makes life-giving, human relationships impossible.

K: Because there seems to be something in a person that won't let him settle for being a package of goods.

J: Well, for me, anyway, there's something in me that won't allow me gladly to spend much time with another person who clearly is a package concealing what's inside.

K: So you're willing to tolerate it long enough to extend the invitation to a different way of being.

J: And it always is an invitation. Moreover, I don't try to sneak it out of them or to shake them up with a well-mastered schedule of reinforcements, aimed to increase the output of authentic talk, because all the time I'm calculating like that, I'm out of touch with the person.

SIDE TWO

K: I know I should pick on you just a little for that, Sid.

J: Go ahead.

K: There's a study by Powell which I think was a doctoral dissertation under your supervision...

J: Absolutely.

K: Which describes the effectiveness of therapist self-disclosure in promoting self-references in almost purely operant terms.

J: Absolutely. That's his dissertation. It was a beautiful one.

K: It's a lovely piece of work, but it certainly looks at the issue from a mechanistic point of view.

J: Well, in a laboratory setting, he wanted to work within the operant paradigm, as close to it as he could produce. He was meticulous, and the operant paradigm appealed to him. He got results showing that authentic responding, true responding out of personal truth, encouraged the subjects in his study.

K: I personally liked the metaphor that authentic self-disclosure is a potent reinforcer.

J: Well, it's also a model.

K: Sure.

J: Nobody's done definitive studies yet to see whether or how modeling invites it and/or reinforces it. Nobody's done a study where before the subject even begins to talk, the researcher does the modeling, and then, in another group, the subject does the talking, and then the reinforcement is offered. Some meticulous researchers might like to try that.

K: I think I'm not meticulous enough for that. I guess I try to do that myself in a group therapy, serve the modeling function—

J: I do.

K: I find it a little frightening.

J: I'm always scared—a little.

K: I'm surprised. I'm doing group therapy now primarily with veterans at a V.A. hospital who are diagnosed as chronic schizophrenic, and wow, the reinforcement or whatever it is that does it, still actually works, although there are some incredible differences in our social backgrounds. If I can get out there and really talk about me, they talk about themselves.

J: That seems to be a truth, doesn't it?

K: Part of life, and maybe this is part of what makes it scary for me, is that the more officially disturbed the patient is, and the more he's distant from me in socio-economic class, the more I really have to get down to bedrock things about sex, love, life, aggression, and death before the sharing begins to catch on both parts. I can't do it on the superficials with somebody who is too far different from me. That's where the big risk comes for me.

J: I think I agree. I'm not sure what is risky for me in advance, but I know that when someone is officially portrayed as radically different from me, I know damn well that at some level of our being, he's not all that different! That we're both human beings and struggling to find some meaningful way to live with our energy, our sexuality, our needs, and our gifts, and there's some basis for common talk between us.

K: I agree. I hear it as a kind of faith statement, but I hear that as part of the faith of a humanist, that there's a real unity about all human beings, and you can operate from that basis.

J: I think it's more than a word, it's a faith. But it's a faith that, for me, is not blind, but is grown out of lived experience, in laboratories, clinics, consulting rooms, a great deal of travel, and a great deal of reading. I read about, let's say, the people who have gone among the Eskimos. The Royal Canadian Mounted Police would have one perspective on the Eskimos who are so different from them, and then I read Farley Mowat accounts of the Caribou Eskimos. The officials saw them as those simple, native people who are happy all the time and couldn't see anything in common between themselves and those Eskimos. But Vilhjalmur Stefansson and Knud Rasmusen and Farley Mowat went to live among them and eat raw meat, almost as anthropologists, and saw that there were differences, yes, but basic commonalities so that one group becomes a metaphor for another.

K: M-hm. So that there's a kind of common humanness and it's a matter of language differences, not in the sense, necessarily, of vocabulary, but cultural forms. If I translate the cultural forms, the metaphor, the outward expression of another group, then I'll face what we have in common. And if there's something about them that I don't want to know about *me*, I'm probably never going to discover it.

J: I think that's true, because whatever, let's say, I see in another person or in another society, is a possibility of mine.

K: Right.

J: Because he's human and I'm human, and if I don't regard it as my possibility, I'm going to be afraid or contemptuous of him. I think that anthropological training for field work is probably an important part of the liberal education and certainly for the training or actually the *untraining* of a psychotherapist, so that he can begin to look at another person as a possibility of himself.

K: There's a real danger, isn't there, of turning things like training and teaching into dirty words, because of all the stuff that's been done under those names.

J: Yes. Well, I think it's a case of context. To be trained as an athlete, trained as a soldier, is one thing. To be trained as someone who is trying to help another person find his way to live effectively and meaningfully, is a kind of training that is largely undoing the effects of training with which a person is indoctrinated in order to be a citizen or an upward, mobile, conforming member of his society.

K: But maybe just to meet my own needs, the thing I hear you emphasizing again and again that matters to me, is the theme of choice. I guess I see in my main goal as a psychotherapist for others is to give them a sense of increased choice, greater freedom of choice. A line in Freud that got to me is from his autobiographical study, "The aim of psychoanalysis is to replace a symptom by an act of choice. Symptom is the opposite of choice."

J: "Where id was, there shall ego be," is another way he said it.

K: Ego is choice.

J: Yes. and I use modern idiom—"Better to be able to swing both ways than to be stuck on one of them." That's something peculiarly cultural about the US, as I've discovered, and I think about Canada, too, and it's the sort of a built-in or trained-in incapacity for dialectical thinking. I see it most clearly in my writing about self-disclosure, which became popular. People said, "Oh my goodness! Non-disclosure is bad. Disclosure is good. So let us then disclose." With the same compulsivity. Of course, what I see as desirable is to be able to be utterly open in relevance and to be utterly private in relevance, to be able to swing both ways. And that's true of every other polarity.

K: I want to put in a plug for my favorite book of yours, *Disclosing Man to Himself.*

J: *Disclosing Man* came out in 1968. It represents the growth of my own experience and the really profound effect I've experienced from being in England for a year and getting acquainted with Ronald Laing, Aaron Hesterson, David Cooper and Paul Zendt. Also to some extent, the European intellectual scene which confirmed me no end. I don't think it taught me a lot positively, but it sure confirmed me to grope and find my own message and to say it in my own ways. And in *Disclosing Man*, I said some things that just weren't being said in American psychology.

K: I hear you saying you can help somebody experience the fact that there are a variety of truths, a variety of possibilities, but he has to test them out and choose for himself. So the way to locate the false prophets is to find the men who say there's one truth, and, baby, this is it, and tough luck if you want another.

J: You have to be Jewish, I think, to recognize false prophets. When someone is really merchandising authority with an implicit way of life, then they are a false prophet, and I think they don't encourage people to grow.

K: Well, who's to knock 4,000 years of accumulated experience in identifying false prophets?

J: Yes, I would never knock it. ▼

* * *

Commentary

SIDNEY JOURARD, YOU ARE THE MAN! In the clearest language, he addressed simple, yet critical elements of the therapeutic relationship. Honesty, truth, and authenticity are such vital components to fostering the healing relationship. Second, Jourard clearly outlined the journey of a young therapist which included: getting in touch with one's own craziness, understanding that we all start by mimicking our elders/supervisors, the criticalness of finding one's own signature, and understanding the commonality of our lives and the lives of our clients.

Jourard's notion of self-disclosure and the significance of bringing that into the consultation room are not for the purpose of showing up the client. Transparency is for communicating to them that you are not past a particular juncture in your life. It is to equate the life experience of two human beings sitting together grappling to discover their authentic selves. Good therapists must know this journey themselves to illuminate the path that another must traverse. And no judgment should be rendered upon the other's journey prior to showing up in therapy or during the therapeutic encounter.

Arriving at a place in life where we are comfortable in our own skin is a milestone of any therapeutic process for either participant. In this way, we are not fulfilling the legacy or destiny of our training at the hands of our parents or supervisors. We are searching, in the present, for those attributes and feelings that define us, in a genuine capacity, both within and outside of our workspace. Jourard stresses that if this genuineness is realized, there will be no difference in therapists' presentation in any aspect of their lives. If duplicity in character exists, Jourard postulates that the therapist will be less helpful, effective, and unable to model for clients. I would add that this incongruence could be grounds for the therapist developing burnout and/or going crazy. Being trapped in an inauthentic persona leads to dishonesty, lack of authenticity, and self-annihilation. Presenting our true selves with others, as Jourard suggests, is an authentic way of being in the world. It models for our clients and serves them in their quest to find their own personal truth or persona.

I loved the clarity yet simplicity of Jourard's language in which he explained his version of the core ingredients of the therapeutic dialogue. He defined self-disclosure as "just another name for speaking the truth to another person." For me, if truth and transparency abound in our relationships, then relationships will flourish. Mutuality, trust, and openness will be the result of that transparency. A genuine engaged encounter can then be attained. Within this encounter, client and therapist will have the possibility of openly sharing those events, feelings, and shame that dwell in the darkness of each of their lives. Therapist sharing, so often left unspoken in psychotherapy, is a key to effective treatment. The development of a therapeutic relationship based on self-disclosure, truth, and genuineness will serve to validate both people. And it will foster a more affirming and less judgmental relationship for the client.

Jourard understood volumes about the quintessential elements of quality psychotherapy. He stressed that it was the result of a solid relationship between two human beings. I think he expressed clearly the importance of breaking down the distance between the therapeutic participants that was a founding principal of psychotherapy in the first half of the 20th century. He realized that sharing common ground and developing a relationship between two human beings based on trust, commonality, and openness would serve to diminish the distance between the chairs and was a key ingredient in helping the client gain self-understanding and freedom. This would provide clients with the opportunity to choose alternatives in living and escape the well-worn patterns and constructs that brought them to the consultation room in the first place.

So, one more time, Sidney Jourard, you da man!

—Robert Rosenblatt, PhD

The Dangerous Case of Donald Trump: 27 Psychiatrists and Mental Health Experts Assess a President

Elizabeth Field

CHARLOTTE, NORTH CAROLINA
clt.therapy.elizabethfield@gmail.com

Book Review

*The Dangerous Case of
Donald Trump:
27 Psychiatrists and
Mental Health Experts
Assess a President*
Edited by Bandy Lee,
MD, MDiv
St. Martin's Press
New York
2017, 360 pages

THIS BOOK IS A COLLECTION OF ESSAYS BY 27 PSYCHIATRISTS AND OTHER MENTAL HEALTH EXPERTS arguing the case that the threat represented by Donald Trump's behavior rises to the standard of our moral and ethical professional "duty to warn," superseding the prevailing Goldwater prohibition against expressing diagnostic opinions about public figures.

The book is divided into three parts. The first section takes on the psychological symptoms of our current president, viewing through clinical language what nonclinical folks view, and some dismiss, as "crazy," "locker room talk," "lying," or "alternative facts." While the writers acknowledge that they have not interviewed Mr. Trump for a formal mental health assessment, they posit that his long tenure in the public eye, combined with his actions since taking office, including his constant Twitter feed, provide a surplus of behavioral information. The authors evaluate this evidence against general diagnostic criteria for malignant narcissism, sociopathy, delusional disorder, dementia, and related traits and disorders. Differing in their emphasis, all of the authors agree that something is very wrong with this subject and that Trump has clearly shown himself to be dangerous. Lance Dodes, MD, of Harvard Medical School, for example, cites Trump's severe sociopathic traits.

The second section of the book describes the psychological community's dilemma, torn between conflicting professional and ethical standards of confidentiality, focusing on strengths to facilitate people's rise to their full potential despite their pathology, the Goldwater prohibition against diagnosing political leaders' character flaws absent formal assessment, and our duty to warn those whom we believe to be in direct danger. This includes the duty to protect the person with the illness, who would inflict the damage to our community (or other) but cannot see his or her own behavior as destructive. What a privileged position and great responsibility we have in our profession.

The last section of the book explores what they coin as "the Trump effect," the impact of his behavior on the public. As Trump took office, many immigrants and people of color or certain religious practices felt fear or terror.

Many of us who care about immigrants and subjugated populations in our country felt fear for their safety if not for our own. Increased anxiety was felt by many, especially victims of bullying, sexual assault, or other trauma, and marginalized groups, including women. After the election, there was a noted increase in racial and religious bullying and assaults, as angry White Americans felt emboldened by the call to "make America great again" to act out their hate crimes. Hate groups like the KKK and Neo-Nazis resurged, and White supremacists gathered in Charlottesville, VA, to rally their cause. This gave rise to the discussion on relativism and truth, given our president's remarks regarding the "violence on both sides." Fueled by disbelief and horror, some in our country have responded with good will, activated to get involved and make Americans proud again.

For obvious reason, I did not take the nomination of Trump to the Republican leader seriously. Perhaps, as I learned from this book, it is my own narcissism and tribal allegiances that allowed me to bury my head in the sand. I wanted to believe the best person for the job would win. I wanted to pretend all was well when this very flawed character bid himself to lead our country. To reconcile my certainty that Hillary Clinton, the Senate, or our judicial system would rescue me from this bad dream, I have read many books trying to explain how we got here as a nation. This book was helpful in grounding me to our professional double bind of silence and responsibility. The book offers some of our field's best scholars and authors opining on Trump's clinical symptoms that baffle nonclinical people but are a familiar lexicon to us. It also highlights our awesome privilege to discern for our country what appears to be a large gap in the vetting process of American presidents. We cannot afford to repeat this mistake by not closing this gap. It is more obvious now than ever that the president needs psychological soundness to do this profoundly dignified, influential, and most stressful job well. Therefore, our community would do well to consider how we can help reduce the stigma of psychological issues and make them on par with general medical health. One step is offering up the courage to see ourselves as potentially the cure to this insanity we have had to accept and integrate as reality.

Another author in this incredible book is an attorney in Florida, who details his attempts to file petitions with the court prior to the election stating his opinion that Trump was or might be psychologically incapacitated to seek or retain employment based on actions supporting diagnoses of histrionic personality disorder and narcissistic personality disorder. James Herb, Esq., wrote that the first judge recused himself and the second dismissed the case. At the time of publication, Herb was still appealing his petition on the grounds of Trump's well documented delusions, gaslighting, and poor judgments in enactment of illegal immigration practices.

Attorney Herb states there is a way out of this reality if we could use the 25th Amendment, which allows the president to give his power over voluntarily to his vice president, as did George W. Bush during a health crisis. There is also an involuntary method of giving presidential power over to the vice president. It would take (a Democratic) Congress and the vice president having the necessary information we can offer as to the inherent danger of an amoral, impulsive, vengeful character running the "free world." This structure is in place and has never been used, but isn't now the time? Can we activate? We know that history repeats itself until we learn from our mistakes and change how we operate. I think it is time to change. As Mahatma Gandhi states, can we be the change we want to see? ▼

Factfulness: Ten Reasons We're Wrong About the World—and Why Things Are Better Than You Think

Scott Gilkeson

TAKOMA PARK, MARYLAND
gilkesons@acm.org

Book Review

Factfulness: Ten Reasons We're Wrong About the World—and Why Things Are Better Than You Think
by Hans Rosling with Ola Rosling and Anna Rosling Ronnlund
Flatiron Books
New York
2018, 255 pages

HOW MUCH DO YOU KNOW ABOUT THE WORLD? TRY THIS SHORT QUIZ:

1. In all low-income countries across the world today, how many girls finish primary school?
   a. 20%
   b. 40%
   c. 60%

2. How many of the world's 1-year-old children today have been vaccinated against some disease?
   a. 20%
   b. 50%
   c. 80%

3. In 1996, tigers, giant pandas, and black rhinos were all listed as endangered. How many of these three species are more critically endangered today?
   a. Two
   b. One
   c. None

Hans Rosling, who died in 2017, spent the last 20 years of his life educating people about the world we live in. He became famous, at least in the data world, giving popular TED talks (viewed more than 35 million times) and lecturing many of the world's most educated and influential people. He usually started his talks with a quiz like the one above (taken from the book), and claims that across all audiences and all countries, only 10% of people score better on these questions than chimpanzees would (assuming their answers would be random). Check at the end of this review to see if you are part of that 10% by having chosen more than one correct answer.

In this delightful and surprising book, Rosling, with son Ola and daughter-in-law Anna, challenge your understanding of our world. But more importantly, they offer 10 tools to help you be more mindful and curious when contemplating our current state. And, as the subtitle says, "things are better than you think."

The Roslings assure us they are not denying there are real problems and areas where things are getting worse, but in general people fail to see that things are steadily and markedly improving. This is due in part, they claim, to a negativity instinct: "our tendency to notice the bad more than the good" (p. 48). For each instinct they identify, they give a short list of counter-strategies. For example, to control the negativity instinct, we should expect bad news. They add (p. 74):

- **Better and bad.** Practice distinguishing between a level (e.g., bad) and a direction of change (e.g., better). Convince yourself that things can be both better and bad.
- **Good news is not news.** Good news is almost never reported. So news is almost always bad. When you see bad news, ask whether equally positive news would have reached you.
- **Gradual improvement is not news.** When a trend is gradually improving, with periodic dips, you are more likely to notice the dips than the overall improvement.
- **More news does not equal more suffering.** More bad news is sometimes due to better surveillance of suffering, not a worsening world.
- **Beware of rosy pasts.** People often glorify their early experiences, and nations often glorify their histories.

One important framework for understanding the world is that life is very different for people in different financial situations. We have a tendency to think in dichotomies—haves and have nots, developed and developing, rich and poor, "us" and "them," perhaps with a gap in the middle (the gap instinct, number one on the *Factfulness* list). That may have been descriptive 50 years ago, but in 2017 and now, the distinctions between "developed" and "developing" countries are disappearing, and the labels are no longer helpful. The authors suggest thinking of four income levels, labeled simply "Level 1" through "Level 4."

At Level 1, where a billion of the world's people live, you make $1 per day. You have five children and must walk hours, barefoot, to fetch water from a dirty mud hole. But if you are lucky and can grow enough to feed your family and sell some surplus, you can move up to Level 2, making $4 per day. Now you can buy sandals and maybe a bike, and you have a gas stove, so your children can attend school rather than spend the day fetching water and firewood. Roughly 3 billion people live at this level.

With more stability and some education, your children can quadruple your income again, to $16 per day. They might have a cold water tap and reliable electricity. They have a motorbike and a better-paying job at a factory in town. They have joined the 2 billion people at Level 3.

Another leap in income, and we are at Level 4, with about 1 billion of the world's 7 billion people. Now an additional $3 a day makes little difference in our lifestyle, and it's hard to imagine how that could lift someone in extreme poverty to Level 2.

How does this change our understanding? As the Roslings say, "Human history started with everyone on Level 1 ... and most children didn't survive to become parents. Just 200 years ago, 85% of the world population was still at Level 1, in extreme poverty. Today, the vast majority of people are spread out in the middle, across Levels 2 and 3, with the same range of standards of living as people in Western Europe and North America in the 1950s" (p. 38). But our perception is stuck in the past (the *destiny instinct*, chapter 7).

This book is a guide to taking personal responsibility for fact-based thought. With the incredible resources available through the Internet and the instantaneous global reach of media, we pride ourselves on the idea that we are well-informed. But our instincts, which served us well for thousands of years of survival on Level 1, sometimes betray us when faced with facts. We have a tendency to think that past performance implies future results (the *straight line instinct*, chapter 3). We make generalizations that help us cope with abstract ideas, but also hide the details that might alert us to new business opportunities in the emerging markets of Africa (the *generalization instinct*, chapter 6). We tend to look for single causes, be they immigrants or government or greedy businesses, when actually we are usually dealing with complex, interacting systems (the *blame instinct*, chapter 9). And we expect the media to explain the world to us, when that is not their job. Normal conditions are just too boring—newspapers would go out of business if that's what they tried to report.

What I like best about the book is that Hans speaks on a personal level. Each chapter begins with an illustrative episode from his extraordinary life, which spans being a child in post-war Sweden to a medical student in India, a young physician in Mozambique's Nacala district—the only doctor for a population of 300,000—a public health researcher and professor, and an Internet sensation, bringing data to life with the flair and showmanship of a circus performer. The work is truly a collaboration, and Ola and Anna developed the tools, wrote the scripts, and finished the book after Hans died. But it is written in Hans' voice, which is warmly humorous and humble while also energetic and inspiring. In recent years, he traveled the world, speaking with leaders of government and non-governmental organizations, captains of industry, and Nobel laureates—and he gleefully relates that none of those groups did better on his quizzes than the chimpanzees.

(Spoiler alert: you can go online to www.gapminder.org/test/2017 to answer the full complement of 13 questions before reading the answers to these samples.)

The answer to the initial questions, in each case, is C. This is a sample of 13 questions that were asked of 12,000 people in 14 countries in 2017. Excluding the last question, which was about climate change and was answered correctly by 87% of participants, the average score was 2.2 questions right. Eighty percent of respondents did worse than the chimpanzees (who would have randomly answered 4 questions correctly), and 15% did not give a single correct answer. ▼

Steven A. Ingram

WEST CHESTER, OHIO
dringram79@gmail.com

Book Review

*Written Off: Mental
Health Stigma and the
Loss of Human Potential*
by Philip T. Yanos, PhD
Cambridge University
Press
United Kingdom
2018, 222 pages

Written Off: Mental Health Stigma and the Loss of Human Potential

NOTHING STICKS WITH A PERSON LIKE A DIAG-
NOSIS OF MENTAL ILLNESS—INSIDE AND OUT.
Insurance companies and families don't forget, and
individuals often feel marked when any diagnosis is applied. Therein lies the proposition by Philip Yanos, that
the marks of the stigmata become primary and one's
whole personhood is "written off." External systemic
processes in the psychological community unconsciously
promote stigma while trying to deny it. And to add in-
sult to injury, persons receiving a mental health diagnosis internally self-stigmatize. How do we reach into the
central lens with which persons view themselves and help
them adjust their view?

In 222 pages (approximately 30 of those are lists of
references), Yanos manages to show why stigma matters, what it looks like, who does it, and its effect, and
to present several potential models to reduce its impact.
Ambitious, sure. Also, significantly successful. All the
major qualitative (and some quantitative) studies are ref-
erenced—many explained. He outlines the journey of developing the definition, vocabulary, and foundations for
an elusive, yet all-pervasive, concept called "stigma." He
illustrates the history of stigma by describing events from
a global level (the Holocaust of WWII), to a public level (actor Margot Kidder's mental health crisis), to a uni-
versally personal level (comments from research subjects
reporting the experience of receiving discrediting labels
to their personhood rather than helpful descriptions of
their impaired behavior at a given time).

This book reports on the pervasiveness of stigma beyond the bounds of North America. Many studies reflect
information from Asian countries, the Baltic States, England, Germany, Switzerland, and the Czech Republic.
Yanos provides information on the understanding of
mental health stigma within a global context.

Yanos is definitive in his declaration that mental
health stigma is a social justice issue. Answering stigma
is not eradicating symptoms, but eliminating the negative social reaction persons have to those symptoms. For
example, there is compelling evidence that psychotic experiences are part of the human experience: as religious
experience, chemically induced (drugs), acute stress, and
agedness. In many ways, anyone under a certain combi-

nation of factors has the capacity to develop psychotic symptoms. We are all in this together.

The primary reason that stigma is important is because it diminishes people's participation in community life and inhibits them from achieving their full potential as human beings. Stigma is fed by the slippery slope from discrediting actions to discrediting people. In fact, many persons, according to Yanos, develop a mental "illness identity," and therefore, are challenged to move from "patienthood to personhood."

The roots of stigma have a frightening history. Yanos points out that "America's forced sterilization laws directly inspired Germany's new Nazi regime, which created its own sterilization law in 1933" (p. 25). Of course, what followed was the stigma that led to extermination of those marked as *Lebensunwertes Leben*, translated as "life unworthy of life." Even in the United States there is a similar sense called "structural stigma," in which five categories of legal rights of life are restricted on the basis of mental illness: voting, jury duty, holding office, marriage, and parenting.

Yanos accentuates a parallel process involving the political zeitgeist and how researchers have identified a sub-type of conservativism known as "right-wing authoritarianism," which places high value on strong authority figures, upholding traditional values/social norms, and displaying hostility toward undesirable groups. Self-identified conservativism is a "consistent predictor of negative stereotypes toward people with mental illness" (p. 81). Furthermore, those who think mental illness "can only happen to others" are more likely to support stigma (p. 85).

Some research subjects reported that their experience supports the belief that the main job requirement for mental health providers is to "sit there and listen." No engagement necessary. Yanos elaborates that psychiatric training encourages emerging physicians to use the biomedical model as a kind of shield against having to identify too much with persons with mental illness. Only by engagement will stigma be reduced, community involvement be increased by persons with mental illness, and the full potential as human beings be inspired.

Yanos describes four programs to counteract disempowering messages of stigma: 1) Narrative Enhancement and Cognitive Therapy (NECT)—20 sessions; 2) Ending Self-Stigma (ESS)—9 sessions; 3) Anti-Stigma Photovoice—10 sessions; and 4) Honest, Open and Proud—3 sessions of 2 hours. The most meaningful component of these programs is the engagement dimension. Each uses a degree of commitment, writing about one's experience, receiving peer feedback on writing, and taking photos that represent one's experience of stigma. Each of these programs also contains a minor psychoeducational component. Mainly, these programs encourage persons to see their mental health challenges as "a dangerous gift to be cultivated and taken care of rather than something needing to be cured or eliminated...the struggle can be a constructive and growth-producing experience" (p. 158).

This book is a rich garden for understanding stigma, encouraging creative thinking regarding addressing it, and engaging one's own story in a narrative that is a deepening of one's personhood. This is the new manual for navigating the currents of mental health stigma.

▼

Bob Rosenblatt

BOB ROSENBLATT, PHD: "I have been sitting in my chair delivering individual, couples and group psychotherapy since 1974. Every day is a new adventure. I never know what I am going to learn, teach or feel in any given session. This is what keeps me coming back hour after hour—day after day. Supervision and practice consultation for other mental health practitioners in Washington, DC, and Atlanta, Georgia, make up another part of my professional life. When I am not in my office, I relish time with my family, especially my grandchildren; I enjoy traveling with my wife, golfing with friends and, now, writing about lessons learned over the years in practice."

Supervision: Creating a Sanctuary

I HAVE BEEN FACILITATING SUPERVISION GROUPS FOR OVER 25 YEARS. Recently, while leading a supervisory group, I was amazed by the depth of the personal work done by the members of the group—on both an intrapersonal and interpersonal level. I began asking myself questions about how this occurred. This group meets every other month for 6 hours. My first answer was that a safe container had been constructed for all participants. I would be willing to take a modicum of credit for eliciting this dynamic, but I wanted to understand more about its evolution.

Was it that the group has been together for many years? Was it that the membership has been steady for awhile? Was it the level of commitment that the group members brought to the table? The answer to these questions felt like NO. It seemed too easy to make these the foundation of a highly functioning supervisory group.

So I was left with the following questions: What are the quintessential elements of creating the safe container for mental health practitioners in order for them to reveal themselves, their work, and their business practices? How has the group enabled the attendees to expose themselves and their work at such a deep level?

One aspect of this group that has produced this elevated level of exposure has been the expectation that the participants bring clients to the group for live supervision. Talk about the level of vulnerability required by this act! This live supervision is far less attentive to the client and more deeply focused on the therapist. Clients are mostly a mirror through which we can see the interpersonal process as well as the handicraft of the supervisee.

My quest for this Intervision article is to get other supervisors to weigh in with a response to this question: What are the primary ingredients of the supervisory group which allow it to become a sanctuary that stimulates the group to function so effectively?

After this particular group gathering, here were my musings on this question. First, I try to abide by this adage attributed to Alex Redmountain, "Less judgment and more curiosity." I arrived here in my work by believing that each client, whether a patient or supervisee, behaves in a manner that is driven by the following notion: Whatever they do, they do it for the best of all possible reasons. Usually, I do not understand their motivation, but I am consistently interested in discovering their dynamic in a way that their actions make sense for them. The construction of each individual's world and their attendant behavior must feel appropriate. Does this mean that I have no judgments? Hell, NO! My judgments serve to fuel my questions and direct my intervention, with the aim of comprehending how it was totally right for them to live and act in such a manner. I believe that this approach in my groups creates a protected and inviting venue in which to expose oneself and one's work. This non-judgmental environment also encourages the supervisee to dig deeper into the etiology of their actions.

Secondly, I look for the common connections in everyone's work, in an effort to string the group together like Christmas lights. One of Irvin Yalom's curative factors in his seminal work on group psychotherapy was universality. There must be commonalities in the intrapersonal construction of mental health practitioners and in how they are impacted by the work of psychotherapy. I push relentlessly to foster mutuality in the room. Competition is fine, but cooperation and equanimity make a healthier and safer road to traverse. I do not create a pecking order for the therapists in my supervision group. Competition is useful to motivate them in the construction of their practices; however, if not attended to, it can become divisive to the group, hindering an open and caring process. Competition appears to be more automatic than cooperation. Without cooperation, no safe container is attainable.

Thirdly, I attempt to model and create the highest level of empathy in the group. Empathic failure creates negative space between participants. Safety emanates from empathy and permits supervisees to discuss difficult practice issues: client contracts, special client deals, money struggles, collection problems, extending credit, sliding scales, missed sessions, etc. Empathy also creates an environment in which group members can explore their fears of success or failure, their capacity to create a thriving practice, their fears of finding and working with a co-therapist, and the struggles of constructing a group practice. Exposing the kinds of work most frightening to talk about—like erotic counter-transference, insensitivity, greed, sadism, and the vast array of negative reactions to clients—must find its way into the supervisory group process to insure the development of a successful and effective psychotherapist.

Two other ingredients are also important in my initial thoughts on this question of forming the safe container. I expect presence of all the members of the supervision group. What is presence? Bugental (1978) described it as the composition of two elements. The first is inter-subjectivity, which means the capacity to tune into yourself and understand what you are experiencing in that moment in the room. The second element is the capacity for emotional expression. The realization of these two factors brings each and every member into the group room. With all present and accounted for, the group is whole and can function on all cylinders. There is no one hanging back with judgments and contempt for another member. The presence of all makes it safe for all.

Ok, last ingredient and then I am going to leave it to my respondents to weigh in about the missing pieces of my ingredient list. I also require authenticity, an extension of presence. With everyone present and interacting, genuine engagement is the mandate and heart of the process. With this at the core of the group culture, the basis for trust and honesty will be elicited and sustained.

So, let me go back to my primary question for writing this case practice issue. What makes a safe container to further the professional and personal development of the person of the therapist? I know that there are many supervisors out there providing critical training for new therapists. I am aspiring to delineate the "how to" for creating this for mentees. Are the ingredients of the supervision group different than those of therapy groups? What do you agree or disagree with in my list? What would you add to my key components? What are the necessary and sufficient conditions for creating the ideal environment to stimulate and nurture the growth of our supervisees? I am excited by this question and look forward to the responses of my colleagues on this question. *Share the craft!* ▼

References:

Bugental, J. (1978). *Psychotherapy and process: The fundamentals of an existential-humanistic approach* (3rd ed.). New York: McGraw-Hill.

Yalom, I. D. (1995). *The theory and practice of group psychotherapy* (4th ed.). New York: Perseus Books Group.

* * *

Process and Awe

GROUPS ARE POWERFUL. Anyone who has experienced process-oriented groups, for good or ill, knows this to be true. And yet I find myself frequently taken by surprise when a group—in a session or in a series of sessions—goes to a depth that feels immeasurable. Perhaps what I register as surprise is a reaction to the experience of awe, which one can never anticipate, and which feels unique each time it happens. Over decades of running process-based groups of various types—therapy groups, supervision groups, groups at meetings and workshops, and a dream group that I run for therapists—I have had many experiences of the sort Bob describes. These experiences seem ineffable, beyond description or quantification. They often feel channeled rather than created.

There's a tradition in Asia of painters who decline to sign their art, feeling that it isn't they who create it, but rather they serve as a conduit for some universal force that is, truly, the creator. Of course, we can see that these artists spent their lives developing their craft, so it may be possible to stand outside the process and see that there are specific techniques that the artist employs. Similarly, it can be useful to think about how the techniques of group therapy leadership foster the process and make more likely, or perhaps invite in, the sort of experience we're talking about.

Safety is not a gadget; it's a state of mind.

—Eleanor Everet

Safety is the sine qua non for all process-oriented groups to be effective. One might say that the most important tasks of the leader involve safety: establishing the boundary conditions which create the container, modeling the cultural expectations of the group, and challenging breaches of the contract. There are as many specific ways of running effective groups as there are effective group leaders; one must be oneself and find one's own way of putting basic principles into practice.

I think that Bob has enumerated many of the important leader attributes that increase safety in the group—a non-judgmental attitude, supporting and seeking to understand any and all self-disclosures, a stance that prizes curiosity, an effort to increase universality of presented material by inviting members to locate within themselves those affects put before the group, and a presentation of empathy, in which the leader communicates an ability to understand the internal experiences of the other.

It is, as he said, important to be present to, and interested in, whatever comes up in the group. Supervision, especially in groups, is a risky business, especially so in the beginning of the venture. Throughout the experience of a supervision group, but most especially in the beginning, the possibility of shame is present. The type of group we're discussing is, by definition, a place where powerful unconscious and regressive forces are at play. Safety doesn't come from keeping them at bay, but rather from welcoming them into the group. A skillful leader must be able to help the group learn to see how to use these forces in positive ways, how dealing with them can increase group cohesiveness and lead to acceptance by members of each other and themselves.

Do All Roads Lead to Rome?

Psychodynamic supervision has changed over past decades as dynamic psychotherapy has changed. Dynamic psychotherapy has become much more relational and "two-person," and its supervision has changed from a focus on what's happening in the patient to the exploration of how the patient's and the therapist's dynamics interact, as the two co-create a therapeutic relationship. Since supervision has come to comprise aspects of psychotherapy, it's not surprising that there can be deep therapeutic work done in supervision group settings. I'm convinced that there are not infrequent moments that a fly on the wall in my office couldn't be sure whether it was observing a psychotherapy or supervision session, be it in an individual or group setting.

However, if that same fly were to be buzzing around my office for a full session it might notice some significant differences. The psychotherapy session would begin in a fashion that seemed random. A therapy group session might be started by any member talking about anything. The supervision session would probably start with specific case material presented by a member scheduled to present that session, which would then start a process. Once started, the process in each group might look similar, since in whichever setting, it's important to follow wherever the material might lead. Effective supervision has to have the latitude to wander into the gray area between "teach" and "treat." In recent years, the supervision literature has been suggesting that the boundary move more deeply into "treat." In the end, however, the purpose of supervision is to help the supervisee(s) develop into better clinicians. While it can be argued that the way to do that is to work with their internal dynamics, I believe that in supervision it's essential to bring the process back to the context of the case, that is, to use whatever happened in the session (or series of sessions) to help understand, and deal with, the clinical situation that began the process.

If that same fly could follow me around, it might observe some differences in the relationship between me and my supervisee vs. patient. At this point, having pushed this poor fly as far as I can, I'd like to open the window and make my next points without it. I think that there are significant differences in the relationships between therapist-patient and supervisor-supervisee. Briefly, both the therapy and supervision relationships can be thought of as containing three components: the working alliance, the transferential relationship, and the real relationship. While the working alliance is the basis for both psychotherapy and supervision, in my work as a therapist I encourage the transferential elements of the relationship, while as a supervisor I foster the real elements to a greater degree. For example, as a therapist I'm more boundaried, and I encourage regressive elements; I'm less disclosing and I'm more interested in my patients' fantasies about me. As a supervisor, I'm more likely to share stories about my professional experiences, good and bad, and my struggles with my own patients. I try to normalize the therapy experiences of my supervisees and to deemphasize the differences between us. My desire is to help my supervisees develop professionally, to come to see themselves as colleagues. As a result of this I'm more comfortable with my supervisees outside the office than I am with my patients, and I believe the reciprocal is true as well. For example, I feel very comfortable chatting and interacting with supervisees at professional meetings or office open houses, whereas I avoid such contact with patients who are therapists with whom I may overlap in these settings.

Because of these differences, I decline to see people in psychotherapy and supervision simultaneously. It feels that doing so would put both me and the patient-supervisee into ambiguous and confusing roles, and I believe that important opportunities that depend on the delineation of those roles would be lost. It feels important to respect the differences.

—Barry J. Wepman, PhD

Response 2

As I pondered Bob's reflections on the primary ingredients of supervisory groups that allow them to become sanctuaries and highly functioning groups, I thought of the many times that I have witnessed the transformative power of groups. Sometimes growth occurs like a wave crashing into us at the beach, and we are forever changed. At other times, growth is incredibly deliberate as we make infinitesimally small changes that coalesce like drops of rain into a puddle that eventually forms an ocean we couldn't have imagined. The common thread that exists in all my memories of transformative change is the necessary confrontation with shame that precedes it. In my writing, I have tried to convey the necessary and sufficient conditions to allow shame to be safely seen, acknowledged, and worked through in groups.

I believe the foundation of our sanctuary is that we nurture growth with mindful acceptance. Social workers start where the client is. Carl Rogers called it unconditional positive regard. Others call this state of consciousness grace, valuing others even knowing their failings. If we feel valued, we can poke our head up from under the sludge of shame. It is a profound relief to drop our pretenses, confess our worst feelings, and discover that we are still accepted.

Mindful acceptance combined with empathic listening and sensitive curiosity allows us to experience a deep sense of being understood. Feeling understood and accepted allows us the freedom to be more spontaneous and authentic without fearing the loss of others' esteem. This authenticity promotes connections in the group by making visible our commonalities. As we face our fears together, this mutual vulnerability leads to increased trust. Trust enhances the sense of safety in the group and leads to hope that there will be support for working through difficulties that have been avoided.

Shame is especially pernicious in that we feel ashamed of feeling shame and want to keep it a secret. Shame is an acutely self-conscious state. Shame makes us want to put our head down, close our eyes, or run away. Shame is an emotion that shuts us down and isolates us from others. We avoid feeling shame and thus we avoid, diminish, and dissociate crucial parts of ourselves. As shame and avoidance of shame increase, our ability to be vulnerable decreases dramatically. As a group therapist and supervisor, helping the group understand their shared experiences of shame and working through the feelings together has been a very potent way to assist the group in creating safety and a sanctuary for their continued growth. Modeling, teaching, and cultivating non-judgmental empathic curiosity by the leader forms the walls of the sanctuary. This container is needed to welcome, acknowledge, and hold the affect in the moment as experiences are explored.

The leader's and each group member's own internalized sense of shame is the most difficult as it lurks in the unconscious. Competition can emanate from places of shame because we want to avoid feeling "less than" others. Competition must be understood and worked through in the group as another potential manifestation of shame. The leader must maintain vigilance over their own emotion state, so that group members do not get caught up in the internalized shame of the leader. If there is acceptance of ourselves as we are in the group, then there is nothing to compete for—there is no "correct" or "right" way; it is what it is, and we are what we are.

One concept that I find tremendously helpful in normalizing and defusing the power of shame is the concept of "enactments." Enactments are inevitable and essential to both group psychotherapy and group supervision. Enactments arise when we find ourselves in situations that activate unformulated experience, when parts of ourselves are outside of our awareness.

We all have dissociated parts because of our involvement in overwhelming circumstances. The splitting off of traumatic events induces shame from our failure to overcome the "impossible to overcome." The affective storms that arise during enactments are the clue that we are mis-understanding the present in terms of the past. Acknowledging this state and giving ourselves permission to be in this state and ask for the help of the group and the group leader shifts our energy from shame (or defenses from shame) to healing and integration of dissociated parts.

The ability of the group members and the group leader to maintain a mentalizing stance in which the members of the group and the group itself are held in mind during an enactment creates the roof of the sanctuary. Accepting that the roof is co-constructed through our own subjectivities, that it inevitably leaks, and that it can even be lost further diminishes shame and points the way toward cooperation and healing. This interdependence between group members and the group and the leader is the column that supports the roof.

The leader's participation in and creation of enactments must be confronted, acknowledged, and accepted by the group and the leader. The leader is immersed in the risks of being in the group just like the members and is always susceptible to enactment through the activation of unformulated experience. The leader's ability to learn from their own unformulated experience, disclosing such, and teaching the group as it unfolds, establishes a state of integrity or wholeness in the group that can light the sanctuary with the golden glow of wisdom.

Group supervision is not equivalent to a psychotherapy group, though group leaders and members can expect to gain considerable personal knowledge and insight. Creating the envi-ronment that encourages and supports the supervision group and the group leader to experience enactments and work through them in the safe container of our sanctuary is, I believe, what helps us to learn and to heal.

As supervision group leaders, we can help group members overcome their resistance to deal-ing with their shame through our willingness to acknowledge, bear with, and work through our own.

—Rob Williams, LICSW, CGP

Response 3

PSYCHOTHERAPISTS FOR THE MOST PART TEND TO BE HIGHLY RELATIONAL PEOPLE. Many are HSP's (Highly Sensitive People), gifted with high emotional intelligence and powers of empathy. One of the most frequent childhood wounds amongst therapists is how misunder-stood and "ungotten" they felt in their families of origin. They were the overly sensitive kids criticized by their parents for being too emotional, having too many feelings, and not accepting the parents' wisdom on emotional matters. A high percentage of therapists as children defaulted into being the emotional caretakers of parents and siblings who had low capacity for processing their own feelings. Alice Miller's (1979) brilliant book, *The Drama of the Gifted Child*, expli-cates how parents' anxieties and pathological narcissism are absorbed sponge-like by the em-pathic child at the expense of his/her own psychological need to be mirrored and understood by the parent. Parent-child caretaking roles are reversed as the child learns to suspend their needs to express anger, anxiety, and disappointment while empathizing with and containing the parents' emotional needs—early training for the future psychotherapist.

In adulthood, many of these emotionally gifted children develop a hunger for more and better emotional attunement. Many are drawn to psychotherapy and are thrilled to finally feel "gotten" by another emotionally attuned person and to have so much attention paid to their feelings and emotional experience. Group therapy in particular takes on aspects of a sanctuary, a safe place with the shared goal of being one's full authentic self while in relationship with others also oriented towards empathy and connection. Many psychotherapists in particular crave these sanctuary experiences and in the last 5-10 years, led by AAP, our field has seen a surge in the prevalence of process group experiences exclusively for therapists. Many therapist organizations around the country now offer experiential process groups as an integral part of their training and workshops.

As Bob indicated in his introduction, there are a myriad of variables that make any group safe or unsafe for participants to relax their defenses and vulnerably open their hearts and souls for the intense intimacy he describes. In the weekly therapist-only groups that I facilitate, where members bring their high capacity for and need for emotional attunement, with all of the correlated wounds and deprivation, I find a key ingredient to success is the therapist paying close attention, more so than in mainstream groups, to members' here-and-now experience of feeling unheard or misunderstood by other members and, most importantly, by the therapist.

When running a therapist group if the energy seems inexplicably stilted, or when one or two members seem alienated, listless, or bored, an unacknowledged failure in therapist attunement is often the cause. Or when a typically engaged member surprisingly opens a group talking about ending due to money or scheduling issues, it's often the case that s/he felt dropped or unattended to in a previous session. I find that some of the most self-aware and emotionally attuned group members who typically love group and who add and contribute immeasurably can unexpectedly regress to very early ego states when triggered by a therapist misattunement. Their usual insight, curiosity, and verbal capacity disappear as they are triggered into a young state of helplessness and despair.

A brief case example:

Chris missed three groups in a row due to "reasonable planned activities" and upon returning, after apologizing, said he felt it was time to end group due to so many other time obligations with his young family and burgeoning practice and a feeling that he'd accomplished all he set out to in group. During his 4 years in group (he was also in ongoing individual therapy with me over 9 years), Chris had been a leader in getting others to question their motives around thoughts of ending group or not examining their tardiness and absences. Early on, he was an exemplar of openness and deep vulnerability when tearfully sharing his shame around his divorce and rage bouts with his children, particularly poignant given his own shaming and rageful father. After his announcement, I and other group members questioned his absences, which only led him to hunker down in a passive mildly detached mode. The group moved away from him, but later on Trina, who over the years was very close with Chris, turned to him, "Hey Chris, you ok?"
"Yeah, I'm fine," he said without emotion or eye contact.
"Alright, well, just want you to know I miss you," she softly said.
He rustled a bit in his seat, looking at the floor.
Just then a vague memory crept into the back of my mind from Chris' last session:

Alan, the newest group member, had earnestly been trying to "therapize" the other group members (a common defensive maneuver in therapist groups) who were sighing and eye-rolling their displeasure. I feared the next interaction would not be pretty. But Chris intervened and cracked everybody up, "Alan, dude, you sound like a frickin therapist talking to a room full of frickin therapists, ARGHHH, PALEAAASE, GET ME OUTTA HERE." The laughter subsided as Alan's sobs filled the airwaves. Haltingly, tearfully, he shared how scared and insecure he felt in this new group of peers, how he felt total shame at not knowing how to connect, and how exhausted he was of pretending to be the expert in every social encounter. "Thank you," Chris said, "thank you for finally showing up."
Time was running out so I intervened and said to the group, "We have to stop now, but, Alan, I want you to know that was really courageous, it takes guts to acknowledge and work through your shame like that, welcome to the group." The group was smiling and engaged as they filed out, though I thought I noticed Chris avoiding my eye contact.

I shared this memory with the group, and Chris sat up straight, his face looking serious. "You noticed that?" he asked. "Yeah," I nodded, "I was concerned about you, but regrettably I realize I kind of forgot it until now. You had just done amazing work with Alan and for the group, and all I did was praise Alan. I neglected you. I regret that."

Chris looked perplexed and then slowly became tearful, "I feel so weak and wimpy. Why am I tearing up? Why should I care if you notice? I wish I were stronger than this."

And Trina lovingly responded, "Chris, this is your strength, fuck your macho bullshit. You're letting yourself be vulnerable. It's what I love about you and makes me feel close with you. Thank you."

Chris of course knew intellectually from his many years of therapy that this was true, yet in his regressed state after the therapist misattunement he was unable to access this "grown up" knowledge and could only react as the young boy gifted with emotional attunement whose father was harsh, indifferent, and certainly not emotionally attuned. The therapist re-attunement and acknowledgment of a previous error helped the whole group return to safety and trust, and Chris to regain his mature mental capacity.

—Nicholas Kirsch, PhD

References:

Miller, A. (1979). *The drama of the gifted child.* (R. Ward, Trans.). New York: Basic Books.

▼

The Ghost in You:
Psychotherapy and the Art of Grieving
Voices, Summer 2019

> "Embrace your grief, for there your soul will grow."
> —Carl Jung

Deadline for submission:
April 15, 2019
Direct questions and
submissions to the editor,
Carla Bauer, LCSW
crbauer01@bellsouth.net

See Submission
Guidelines on the AAP
website:
www.aapweb.com.

LOSS IS INTEGRAL TO THE HUMAN EXPERIENCE. There is no attachment without the risk and eventuality of loss. The response to loss, however, determines our engagement in the present moment. The ability to navigate grief helps determine the quality and duration of our relationships. Mourning can be a vehicle for, or an obstacle to, growth.

Therapeutic witnessing offers a unique opportunity to metabolize grief, and the echoes of past loss can be a cry to reawaken to life. However, for the therapist and the patient whose unresolved grief has been touched, the work may be excruciating and can create unintended impasses. Dissociation, repression, fragmentation, and somatization can all vie for control. Ultimately, the goal is to integrate and regulate, rather than exorcise, haunted histories.

Consider the theme of grief and ghosts as it relates to the person of the therapist, the therapy process, our community, and the world at large. How do productive responses to loss and grief facilitate growth and development? How do ghosts interfere with mourning and haunt the therapy process? How do dissociation, fragmentation, repression, and somatization inhibit grief work? How does unresolved grief contribute to intergenerational transmission of trauma, haunting individuals, institutions, and communities? How do cultural differences in the understanding of death and grieving rituals impact the metabolism of loss?

Some potential areas of grieving ghosts, in both clients and therapists: relatives and survivors of holocaust and other cultural traumas, conscious and unconscious; illness, aging, death; disabled or ill children; divorce (marital, friendship, co-therapy); life transitions (college, moving away, marriage, retirement); political grief; decision making, commitment, and loss of freedom; group therapy grief (illness, termination); incarceration.

What ethical concerns arise around confidentiality, boundaries, disclosure and other matters when loss and grief enter the therapy relationship? How does attending to the ghosts within our clients trigger our own experiences of loss, and how do the losses in our lives trigger the ghosts within our clients?

Voices welcomes submissions in the form of personal essay, research- and case-based inquiry, poetry, art, cartoons and photography. ▼

The Geometry of Place, The Tangled Roots of Home
Voices, Winter 2019

OUR HISTORIES OF PLACE AND HOME ARE SHARED BY FAMILY AND COMMUNITY AND ARE UNIQUE-LY PERSONAL AT THE SAME TIME. This issue of Voices will explore how the physical, emotional, and psychological dimensions of place and home shape and hold us and make us uniquely who we are as human beings.

Consider: What does the construct of "home" mean to you? How did the landscape of your childhood shape your identity, your psyche, and the rhythms of your life? How did the place you were raised inform your understanding of reality and your values? How did your roots impact your journey into the world beyond home? What has been your experience of leaving home or finding and forming "home" throughout your life? How has your own experience of place and home influenced the milieu you have created or adopted for your work as a therapist?

Consider also the ways in which your clients' unique histories of place and home have shaped their journey, their struggles, and their sense of safety and belonging. How do their histories affect and inform your therapeutic endeavors and your relationship to your clients, whose trajectories toward and away from home inevitably differ from your own?

Voices welcomes submissions in the form of personal essay, research- and case-based inquiry, poetry, art, cartoons and photography.

▼

Deadline for submission:
August 15, 2019
Direct questions and submissions to the editor, Carla Bauer, LCSW
crbauer01@bellsouth.net
or to the guest editors. See Submission Guidelines on the AAP website:
www.aapweb.com

Winter 2019
Guest Editors:
David Pellegrini, PhD
dspellegrini@gmail.com
Tom Burns, PhD
burnsvoices@gmail.com

The American Academy of Psychotherapists invites you to be a part of an enlightening journey into...

VOICES

Voices is a uniquely rewarding publication providing a meeting ground with other experienced psychotherapists. A theme-oriented journal, *Voices* presents personal and experiential essays by therapists from a wide range of orientations. Each issue takes you on an intimate journey through the reflections of therapists as they share their day-to-day experiences in the process of therapy. *Voices'* contributors reveal insights inherent in our lives, our culture and our society.

As a subscriber, you'll have the opportunity to experience contributions from noted luminaries in psychotherapy. Using various styles from articles to poems, *Voices* is interdisciplinary in its focus, reflecting the aims and mission of its publisher, the American Academy of Psychotherapists.

VOICES SUBSCRIPTION

Please start my one-year subscription to AAP's journal *Voices* at $65 for individuals PDF only; $85 for individuals PDF & print copy. Institutional subscriptions may be reserved directly through the AAP office or through the traditional subscription agencies at $249 per year. *Voices* is published electronically three times per year and is delivered to your email address as an ePublication.

Name
Address
City   State   ZIP
Telephone   Fax
Email

❏ My check made payable to AAP *Voices* is enclosed.
❏ Please charge to my credit card, using the information I have supplied below:
Form of payment: ❏ Master Card   ❏ Visa
Account #   Expiration:
Signature

Address all orders by mail to:
Voices
230 Washington Ave Ext, Suite 101
Albany, NY 12203
You may also fax your order to (518) 240-1178.
For further information, please call (518) 694-5360

Voices: The Art and Science of Psychotherapy, is the journal of the American Academy of Psychotherapists. Written by and for psychotherapists and healing professionals, it focuses on therapists' personal struggles and growth and on the promotion of excellence in the practice of psychotherapy. The articles are written in a personalized voice rather than an academic tone, and they are of an experiential and theoretical nature that reflects on the human condition.

Each issue has a central theme as described in the call for papers. Manuscripts that fit this theme are given priority. Final decision about acceptance must wait until all articles for a particular issue have been reviewed. Articles that do not fit into any particular theme are reviewed and held for inclusion in future issues on a space available basis.

Articles. See a recent issue of *Voices* for general style. Manuscripts should be double-spaced in 12 point type and no longer than 4,000 words (about 16 to 18 pages). Do not include the author's name in the manuscript, as all submissions receive masked review by two or more members of the Editorial Review Board. Keep references to a minimum and follow the style of the *Publication Manual of the American Psychological Association, 5th ed.*

Submit via email, attaching the manuscript as a Word document file. Send it to Carla Bauer *(crbauer01@bellsouth.net)*. Put "Voices" in the email's subject line, and in the message include the author's name, title and degree, postal address, daytime phone number, manuscript title, and word count. Please indicate for which issue of *Voices* the manuscript is intended.

If a manuscript is accepted, the author will be asked to provide a short autobiographical sketch (75 words or less) and a photograph that complies with technical quality standards outlined in a PDF which will be sent to you.

Neither the editorial staff nor the American Academy of Psychotherapists accepts responsibility for statements made in its publication by contributors. We expect authors to make certain there is no breach of confidentiality in their submissions. Authors are responsible for checking the accuracy of their quotes, citations, and references.

Poetry. We welcome poetry of high quality relevant to the theme of a particular issue or the general field of psychotherapy. Short poems are published most often.

Book and Film Reviews. Reviews should be about 500 to 750 words, twice that if you wish to expand the material into a mini-article.

Visual Arts. We welcome submissions of photographs or art related to the central theme for consideration. Electronic submissions in JPEG or TIFF format are required. If you would like to submit images, please request the PDF of quality standards from Mary de Wit at *md@in2wit.com* or find it on *www.aapweb.com*. Images are non-returnable and the copyright MUST belong to the submitting artist.

Copyright. By submitting materials to *Voices* (articles, poems, photos or artwork), the author transfers and consents that copyright for that article will be owned by the American Academy of Psychotherapists, Inc. ▾

VISION STATEMENT

Our vision is to be the premier professional organization where therapeutic excellence and the use of self in psychotherapy flourish.

MISSION STATEMENT

The mission of the American Academy of Psychotherapists is to invigorate the psychotherapist's quest for growth and excellence through authentic interpersonal engagement.

CORE VALUES

- Courage to risk and willingness to change
- Balancing confrontation and compassion
- Commitment to authenticity with responsibility
- Honoring the individual and the community

FULL MEMBERSHIP

Full Membership in the Academy requires a doctoral or professional degree in one of the following mental health fields: psychiatry, clinical or counseling psychology, social work, pastoral counseling, marriage and family therapy, counseling, or nursing, and licensure which allows for the independent practice of psychotherapy.

- Specific training in psychotherapy with a minimum of 100 hours of supervision.
- At least one year of full-time post graduate clinical experience (or the equivalent in part-time experience) for doctoral level applicants, at least two years for others.
- A minimum of 100 hours of personal psychotherapy.

A person who does not fulfill the above requirements but who is able to document a reasonable claim for eligibility, such as a distinguished contributor to the field of psychotherapy, may also be considered for full membership.

OTHER CATEGORIES OF MEMBERSHIP

In the interest of promoting the development of experienced psychotherapists, one category of associate membership is offered for those with the intent of becoming full members. These members will be working with a mentor as they progress to Full Membership.

Associate Membership

- has completed a relevant professional degree
- is currently practicing psychotherapy under supervision appropriate to the licensure
- has recommendations from at least three faculty, supervisors, and/or Academy members
- has completed or is actively engaged in obtaining 100 hours of personal psychotherapy
- agrees to work with an Academy member mentor
- may be an associate for no more than five years

Student Affiliate

For students currently enrolled in a graduate degree program. Application includes acceptable recommendations from two faculty, supervisors or Academy members.

For information regarding membership requirements or to request an application, contact the Central Office. Membership information and a printable application form are also available on the Academy's Web site, www.aapweb.com.

EXECUTIVE OFFICES

aap@caphill.com
230 Washington Ave Ext, Suite 101
Albany, NY 12203
Phone (518) 240-1178
Fax (518) 463-8656

2018 OFFICERS

Doug Cohen, PhD
President

Gordon Cohen, PsyD
Immediate Past President

David Donlon, LCSW
President-Elect

Steven Ingram, D Min
Secretary

Philip Spiro, MD
Treasurer

EXECUTIVE COUNCIL

2015 – 2018
Ellen Carr, MSW
Jacob Megdell, PhD

2016 – 2018
Judy Lazarus, MSW

2016 – 2019
Neil Makstein, PhD
Stephanie Spalding, LCSW
Linda Tillman, PhD

2017 – 2020
David Pellegrini, PhD
Lori Oshrain, PhD
Tandy Levine, LCSW

Made in the USA
Middletown, DE
18 July 2020

12154921R00076